TARANTULA

Tarantula | Bob Dylan

THE MACMILLAN COMPANY, NEW YORK, NEW YORK

This is a work of fantasy and imagination.

Library of Congress Catalog Card Number: 66-25502

THIRD PRINTING 1971

The Macmillan Company
866 Third Avenue, New York, N.Y. 10022
Collier-Macmillan Canada Ltd., Toronto, Ontario

Printed in the United States of America

Here Lies Tarantula

In the fall of 1966, we were to publish Bob Dylan's "first book." Other publishers were envious. "You'll sell a lot of copies of *that*," they said, not really knowing what *that* was, except that *it* was by Bob Dylan. A magic name then. "Besides, look how many copies of John Lennon's book were sold. This would be twice as big—maybe more." Didn't matter what was in it.

Bob would visit our offices occasionally. It was hard for him to travel in broad daylight in those times, even to our old 12th Street and Fifth Avenue building, a marvelous structure with a marble staircase and thick walls covered with portraits and photographs of people like W. B. Yeats. We had published his first book too, all his books in fact.

One day when Bob appeared the receptionist at the big oak desk decided she didn't care for the look of him and phoned upstairs to see if it was all right to allow him to enter. It seemed funny then, because there were very few places in which he found himself unwelcome. He would go in and people would look and whisper and stand back. They thought it was poor form to press him. They didn't quite know what to say to him anyway.

We talked about his book, his hopes for it and what he wanted it to look like. And what he wanted to call it. We knew only it was "a work in progress," a first book by a young songwriter, a quickly famous shy boy who sometimes wrote poetry and who was having an odd effect on a lot of us.

We weren't quite sure what to make of the book—except money. We didn't know what Bob was up to. We only knew that good publishers give authors a chance to catch up with themselves. Robert Lowell talks about "free-lancing out along the razor's edge," and we thought Bob was doing some of that.

We worked out a design for the book that we liked. Bob liked it too, and we set it up. We also made up some buttons and shopping bags with a picture of Bob and the word *Tarantula*. We wanted to call everyone's attention to the fact that the book was being published. We wanted to help *Life* and *Look* and *The New York Times* and *Time* and *Newsweek* and all the rest who were talking about Bob. We brought a set of galleys to him so he could take one last good look at it before we printed it and bound it and started to fill all the orders that had come in.

It was June. Bob took a break from some film-editing he was doing. We talked a little about the book and about Rameau and Rimbaud and Bob promised to finish "making a few changes" in two weeks. A few days after that Bob stopped working. A motorcycle accident had forced him into a layoff.

The book might have been published just the way it had been left. But we could not do that. Bob did not want that. Now he was not ready to "make the changes." It was nothing more than that.

Time went by and the year came to an end. Some people were furious. Where was this so-called book? He had promised. The Macmillan Company had promised. They even had made those buttons and shopping bags, and there were some left over that people were snitching from the warehouse and selling because they had Bob's picture on them and maybe a picture would be better than the book anyway.

There were also a few sets of galleys that had gone around to different people who were being given a preview of the book. These advance review galleys are made of every book. Sometimes they are loose and sometimes they are bound up with a spiral binding.

More time went by. There were still many people who talked about the book and wondered when it would come out. But it couldn't come out unless or until Bob wanted it to. He didn't.

The more time that went by, the more curious and furious some people became. Doesn't matter that it's his work, they said. Doesn't matter what he wants, they said. What right has he got anyway. And so they managed to get hold of a copy or two of those galleys and they started to make some copies of the copies. They sold even better than the buttons had.

Some newspapers saw that this was happening and decided to print parts of the book and long reviews and speculations and denunciations. Bob didn't like this idea and neither did we. We know that an artist has the right to make his own decisions about what happens to his work. And a publisher should protect this right, not abrogate it. Everyone should know this. You don't take what doesn't belong to you, and the only thing that truly belongs to us is our work.

Poets and writers tell us how we feel by telling us how they feel. They find ways to express the inexpressible. Sometimes they tell the truth and sometimes they lie to us to keep our hearts from breaking.

Bob has always been out ahead, working in ways which can be hard to understand. A lot of what he wrote then in *Tarantula* doesn't seem so hard to understand now. People change and their feelings change. But *Tarantula* hasn't been changed. Bob wants it published and so it is now time to publish it. This is Bob Dylan's first book. It is the way he wrote it—and now you know.

The Publisher

TARANTULA

Guns, the Falcon's Mouthbook
& Gashcat Unpunished

aretha/ crystal jukebox queen of hymn & him diffused in drunk transfusion wound would heed sweet soundwave crippled & cry salute to oh great particular el dorado reel & ye battered personal god but she cannot she the leader of whom when ye follow, she cannot she has no back she cannot . . . beneath black flowery railroad fans & fig leaf shades & dogs of all nite joes, grow like arches & cures the harmonica battalions of bitter cowards, bones & bygones while what steadier louder the moans & arms of funeral landlord with one passionate kiss rehearse from dusk & climbing into the bushes with some favorite enemy ripping the postage stamps & crazy mailmen & waving all rank & familiar ambition than that itself, is needed to know that mother is not a lady . . . aretha with no goals, eternally single & one step soft of heaven/ let it be understood that she owns this melody along with her emotional diplomats & her earth & her musical secrets

the censor in a twelve wheel drive semi
stopping in for donuts & pinching the
waitress/ he likes his women raw & with

syrup/ he has his mind set on becoming
a famous soldier

manuscript nitemare of cut throat high & low & behold the
prophesying blind allegiance to law fox, monthly cupid &
the intoxicating ghosts of dogma . . . nay & may the boat-
men in bathrobes be banished forever & anointed into the
shelves of alive hell, the unimaginative sleep, repetition
without change & fat sheriffs who watch for doom in the
mattress . . . hallaluyah & bossman of the hobos cometh
& ordaining the spiritual gypsy davy camp now being infil-
trated by foreign dictator, the pink FBI & the interrogating
unknown failures of peacetime as holy & silver & blessed
with the texture of kaleidoscope & the sandal girl . . . to
dream of dancing pillhead virgins & wandering apollo at
the pipe organ/ unscientific ramblers & the pretty things
lucky & lifting their lips & handing down looks & regards
from the shoulders of adam & eve's minstrel peekaboo . . .
passing on the chance to bludgeon the tough spirits & the
deed holders into fishlike buffoons & yanking ye erratic
purpose . . . surrendering to persuasion, the crime against
people, that be ranked alongside murder & while doctors,
teachers, bankers & sewer cleaners fight for their rights,
they must now be horribly generous . . . & into the march
now where tab hunter leads with his thunderbird/ pearl
bailey stomps him against a buick & where poverty, a per-

fection of neptune's unused clients, plays hide & seek &
escaping into the who goes there? & now's not the time to
act silly, so wear your big boots & jump on the garbage
clowns, the hourly rate & the enema men & where junior
senators & goblins rip off tops of question marks & their
wives make pies & go now & throw some pies in the face &
ride the blinds & into aretha's religious thighs & movement
find ye your nymph of no conscience & bombing out your
young sensitive dignity just to see once & for all if there
are holes & music in the universe & watch her tame the sea
horse/ aretha, pegged by choir boys & other pearls of
mamas as too gloomy a much of witchy & dont you know
no happy songs

    the lawyer leading a pig on a leash
    stopping in for tea & eating the censor's
    donut by mistake/ he likes to lie about
    his age & takes his paranoia seriously

the hospitable grave being advertised & given away in
whims & journals the housewife sits on. finding herself
financed, ruptured but never censored in & also never flush-
ing herself/ she denies her corpse the courage to crawl—
close his own door, the ability to die of bank robbery &
now catches the heels of old stars making scary movies on

her dirt & her face & not everybody can dig her now. she
is private property . . . bazookas in the nest & weapons of
ice & of weatherproof flinch & they twitter, make scars &
kill babies among lady shame good looks & her constant foe,
tom sawyer of the breakfast cereal causing all females pay-
ing no attention to this toilet massacre to be hereafter
called LONZO & must walk the streets of life forever with
lazy people having nothing to do but fight over women
. . . everybody knows by now that wars are caused by
money & greed & charity organizations/ the housewife is
not here. she is running for congress

> the senator dressed like an austrian
> sheep. stopping in for coffee & insulting
> the lawyer/ he is on a prune diet &
> secretly wishes he was bing crosby
> but would settle for being a close
> relative of edgar bergen

passing the sugar to iron man of the bottles who arrives
with the grin & a heatlamp & he's pushing "who dunnit"
buttons this year & he is a love monger at first sight . .
you have seen him sprout up from a dumb hill bully into a
bunch of backslap & he's wise & he speaks to everyone as if
they just answered the door/ he dont like people that say

he comes from the monkeys but nevertheless ne is dull & he
is destroyingly boring . . . while Allah the cook scrapes
hunger from his floor & pounding it into the floating dishes
with roaring & the rest of the meatheads praising each
other's power & argue over acne & recite calendars & point-
ing to each other's garments & liquid & disperse into seg-
ments & die crazy deaths & bellowing farce mortal farm
vomit & why for Jesus Christ be Just another meathead?
when all the tontos & heyboy lose their legs trying to frug
while kemosabe & mr palladin spend their off hours remain-
ing separate but equal & anyway why not wait for laughter
to straighten the works out meantime & WOWEE smash
& the rage of it all when former lover cowboy hanging up-
side down & Suzy Q. the angel putting new dime into this
adoption machine as out squirts a symbol squawking &
freezing & crashing into the bowels of some hideous soap
box & it's a rumble & iron man picking up his "who dunnit"
buttons & giving them away free & trying to make friends
& even tho youre belonging to no political party, youre now
prepared, prepared to remember something about some-
thing

the chief of police holding a bazooka
with his name engraved on it. coming in
drunk & putting the barrel into the face
of the lawyer's pig. once a wife beater,

he became a professional boxer & received
a club foot/ he would literally like to
become an executioner. what he doesnt know
is that the lawyer's pig has made friends
with the senator

gambler's passion & his slave, the sparrow & he's ranting
from a box of black platform & mesmerizing this ball of
daredevils to stay in the morning & dont bust from the fac-
tories/ everyone expecting to be born with whom they love
& theyre not & theyve been let down, theyve been lied to
& now the organizers must bring the oxen in & dragging
leaflets & gangrene enthusiasm, ratfinks & suicide tanks from
the pay phones to the housing developments & it usually
starts to rain for a while . . . little boys cannot go out &
play & new men in bulldozers come in every hour deliver-
ing groceries & care packages being sent from las vegas . . .
& nephews of the coffee bean expert & other favorite sons
graduating with a pompadour & cum laude—praise be & a
wailing farewell to releasing the hermit & beautifully ugly
& fingering eternity come down & save your lambs &
butchers & strike the roses with its rightful patsy odor . . .
& grampa scarecrow's got the tiny little wren & see for your-
self while saving him too/ look down oh great Romantic.
you who can predict from every position, you who know
that everybody's not a Job or a Nero nor a J.C. Penney . . .

look down & seize your gambler's passion, make high wire
experts into heroes, presidents into con men. turn the even-
tual . . . but the hermits being not talking & lower class or
insane or in prison . . . & they dont work in the factories
anyway

>the good samaritan coming in with the
>words "round & round we go" tattooed on
>his cheek/ he tells the senator to stop
>insulting the lawyer/ he would like to
>be an entertainer & brags that he is
>one of the best strangers around, the
>pig jumps on him & starts eating his
>face

illiterate coins of two head wrestling with window washer
who's been reincarnated from a garden hoe & after once
being pushed around happily & casually hitting a rock once
in a while is now bitter hung up on finding some inferior.
he bites into the window ledge & by singing "what'll we do
with the baby-o" to thirsty peasant girls wanting a drink
from his pail, he is thinking he is some kind of success but
he's getting his kicks telling one of the two headed coins
that tom jefferson used to use him around the house when

the bad stuff was growing . . . the lawrence welk people inside the window, theyre running the city planning division & they hibernate & feeding their summers by conversing with poor people's shadows & other ambulance drivers, & they dont even notice this window washer while the families who tell of the boogey men & theyre precious & there's pictures of them playing golf & getting blacker & they wear oil in the window washer's union hall & these people consider themselves gourmets for not attending charlie starkweather's funeral ye gads the champagne being appropriate pagan & the buffalo, tho the restaurant owners are vague about it, is fast disappearing into violence/ soon there will be but one side of the coin & mohammed wherever he comes from, cursing & window washers falling & then no one will have any money . . . broad save the clean, the minorities & liberace's countryside.

the truck driver coming in with a carpet
sweeper under his eyes/ everybody says
"hi joe" & he says "joe the fellow that
owns this place. i'm just a scientist. i
aint got no name" the truck driver hates
anybody that carries a tennis racket/ he
drinks all the senator's coffee & proceeds
to put him in a headlock

first you snap your hair down & try to tie up the kicking
voices on a table & then the sales department people with
names like Gus & Peg & Judy the Wrench & Nadine with
worms in her fruit & Bernice Bearface blowing her brains
on Butch & theyre all enthused over locker rooms & vege-
tables & Muggs he goes to sleep on your neck talking shop
& divorces & headline causes & if you cant say get off my
neck, you just answer him & wink & wait for some morbid
reply & the liberty bell ringing when you dont dare ask
yourself how do you feel for God's sake & what's one
more face? & the difference between a lifetime of goons &
holes, company pigs & beggars & cancer critics learning
yoga with raving petty gangsters in one act plays with
V-eight engines all being tossed in the river & combined in
a stolen mirror . . . compared to the big day when you
discover lord byron shooting craps in the morgue with his
pants off & he's eating a picture of jean paul belmondo & he
offers you a piece of green lightbulb & you realize that
nobody's told you about This & that life is not so simple
after all . . . in fact that it's no more than something to
read & light cigarettes with . . . Lem the Clam tho, he
really gives a damn if dale really does get nailed slamming
down the scotch & then going outside with Maurice, who
aint the Peoria Kid & dont look the same as they do in Des
Moines, Iowa & good old debbie, she comes along & both
her & dale, they start shacking up in the newspapers & jesus

who can blame 'em? & Amen & oh lordy, & how the parades
dont need your money baby . . . it's the confetti & one
george washington & Nadine who comes running & says
where's Gus? & she's salty about the bread he's been making
off her worms while dollars becoming pieces of paper . . .
but people kill for paper & anyway you cant buy a thrill
with a dollar as long as pricetags, the end of the means &
only as big as your fist & they dangle from a pot of golden
rainbow . . . which attacks & which covers the saddles of
noseless poets & wonder blazing & somewhere over the rain-
bow & blinding my married lover into the ovation maniacs/
cremating innocent child into scrapheap for vicious con-
troversy & screwball & who's to tell charlie to stop & not
come back for garbage men arent serious & they gonna get
murdered tomorrow & next march 7th by the same kids &
their fathers & their uncles & all the rest of these people that
would make leadbelly a pet . . . they will always kill gar-
bage men & wiping the smells but this rainbow, she goes off
behind a pillar & sometimes a tornado destroys the drug-
stores & floods bring polio & leaving Gus & Peg twisted in
the volleyball net & Butch hiding in madison square garden
. . . Bearface dead from a flying piece of grass! I.Q.—some-
where in the sixties & twentieth century & so sing aretha
. . . sing mainstream into orbit! sing the cowbells home!
sing misty . . . sing for the barber & when youre found
guilty of not owning a cavalry & not helping the dancer
with laryngitis . . . misleading valentino's pirates to the

indians or perhaps not lending a hand to the deaf pacifist in
his sailor jail . . . it then must be time for you to rest &
learn new songs . . . forgiving nothing for you have done
nothing & make love to the noble scrubwoman

what a drag it gets to be. writing
for this chosen few. writing for any-
one cpt you. you, daisy mae, who are
not even of the masses . . . funny thing,
tho, is that youre not even dead yet . . .
i will nail my words to this paper,
an fly them on to you. an forget about
them . . . thank you for the time.
youre kind.
love an kisses
your double
Silly Eyes (in airplane trouble)

Having a Weird Drink with the Long Tall Stranger

back betty, black bready blam de lam! bloody had a baby blam de lam! hire the handicapped blam de lam! put him on the wheel blam de lam! burn him in the coffee blam de lam! cut him with a fish knife blam de lam! send him off to college & pet him with a drumstick blam de lam! boil him in the cookbook blam de lam! fix him up an elephant blam de lam! sell him to the doctors blam de lam . . . back betty, big bready blam de lam! betty had a milkman, blam de lam! sent him to the chain gang blam de lam! fixed him up a navel, blam de lam (hold that tit while i git it. Hold it right there while i hit it . . . blam!) fed him lotza girdles, raised him in pneumonia . . . black bloody, itty bitty, blam de lam! said he had a lampchop, blam de lam! had him in a stocking, stuck artichokes in his ears, planted him in green beans & stuck him on a compass blam de lam! last time i seed him, blam de lam! he was standing in a window, blam de lam! hundred floors up, blam de lam! with his prayers & his pig-foot, blam de lam! black betty, black betty blam de lam! betty had a loser blam de lam, i spied him on the ocean with a long string of muslims—blam de lam! all going quack quack . . . blam de lam! all going quack quack. blam!

13

sorry to say, but i'm going
to have to return your ring.
it's nothing personal, excpt
that i cant do a thing with
my finger & it's already
beginning to smell like an
eyeball! you know, like i like
to look weird, but nevertheless,
when i play my banjo on stage, i
have to wear a glove. needless
to say, it has started to affect
my playing. please believe me.
it has nothing whatsoever to
do with my love for you . . .
in fact, sending the ring back
should make my love for you
grow all the more profound . . .
        say hi to your doctor
        love,
        Toby Celery

(Pointless Like a Witch)

trip into the light here abraham . . . what about this boss
of yours? & dont tell me that you just do what youre told!
i might not be hip to your sign language but i come in peace.
i seek knowledge. in exchange for some information, i will
give you my fats domino records, some his an hers towels
& your own private press secretary . . . come on. fall
down here. my mind is blank. i've no hostility. my eyes are
two used car lots. i will offer you a cup of urn cleaner—we
can learn from each other/ just dont try & touch my kid

        got too drunk last nite. musta drunk
        too much. woke up this morning with
        my mind on freedom & my head feeling
        like the inside of a prune . . . am
        planning to lecture today on police
        brutality. come if you can get away.
        see you when you arrive. write me
        when youre coming
                        your friend,
                        homer the slut

Ballad in Plain Be Flat

the feet were stuck between the petticoat & tom dick &
harry rode by & they all screamed . . . her lips was so
small & she had trenchmouth & when i saw what i had
done, i guard my face/ the time is handled by some crazy
cheerleader snob & sticking her tongue out, dropping a
purple tostle cap, she mingles with a bus, caresses a bloody
crucifix & is praying for her purse to be stolen up gunpow-
der alley! her name, Delia, she envies the block of chain &
kingdom where the khaki thermometer kid, obviously a
front man & getting a commission growling "she'll drown
you! split your eyes! put your mind where your mouth is!
see it explode! just 65 & she dont mind dying!" is bending
over for scraps of food, fighting an epileptic fit & trying to
keep dry in a typical cincinnati weather . . . Claudette,
the sandman's pupil, wounded in her fifth year in the busi-
ness & she's only 15 & go ahead ask her what she thinks of
married men & governors & shriner conventions go ahead
ask her & Delia, who's called Debra when she walks around
in her nurse uniform, she casts off pure light in the cellar &
has principles/ ask her for a paper favor & she gives you a
geranium poem . . . chicago? the hogbutcher! meat-
packer! whatever! who cares? it's also like cleveland! like
cincinnati! i gave my love a cherry. sure you did. did she

tell you how it tasted? what? you also gave her a chicken?
fool! no wonder you want to start a revolution

    look. i dont care what your daddy
    says. j. edgar hoover is just not that
    good a guy. like he must have infor-
    mation on every person inside the
    white house that if the public knew
    about, could destroy those people/
    if any of the knowledge that he's
    got ever got out, are you kidding,
    the whole country would probably
    quit their jobs & revolt. he aint never
    gonna lose his job. he will resign with
    honor. you just wait & see . . . cant you figure
    out all this commie business for yourself?
    you know, like how long can car thieves
    terrify the nation? gotta go. there's a
    fire engine chasing me. see you when i get
    my degree. i'm going crazy without you.
    cant see enough movies
                                    your crippled lover,
                                    benjamin turtle

On Busting the Sound Barrier

the neon dobro's F hole twang & climax from disappointing
lyrics of upstreet outlaw mattress while pawing visiting
trophies & prop up drifter with the bag on head in bed with
next of kin to the naked shade—a tattletale heart & wolf of
silver drizzle inevitable threatening a womb with the open-
ing of rusty puddle, bottomless, a rude awakening & gone
frozen with dreams of birthday fog/ in a boxspring of sadly
without candle sitting & depending on a blemished guide,
you do not feel so gross important/ success, her nostrils
whimper. the elder fables & slain kings & inhale manners of
furious proportion, exhale them against a glassy mud . . .
to dread misery of watery bandwagons, grotesque & vomit-
ing into the flowers of additional help to future treason &
telling horrid stories of yesterday's influence/ may these
voices join with agony & the bells & melt their thousand
sonnets now . . . while the moth ball woman, white, so
sweet, shrinks on her radiator, far away & watches in with
her telescope/ you will sit sick with coldness & in an un-
enchanted closet . . . being relieved only by your dark
jamaican friend—you will draw a mouth on the lightbulb
so it can laugh more freely

forget about where youre bound.
youre bound for a three octave
fantastic hexagram. you'll see
it. dont worry. you are Not bound
to pick wildwood flowers . . . like
i said, youre bound for a three
octave titanic tantagram
                        your little squirrel,
                        Pety, the Wheatstraw

Thermometer Dropping

the original undertaker, Jane, with bangs, & her hysterical
bodyguard, Coo, who comes from Jersey & always carries
his lunch/ they screech around the corner & tie the old
buick into a lamppost/ along came three bachelors sprin-
kling the sidewalk with fish/ they spot the mess. first bach-
elor, Constantine, he winks at second bachelor, Luther, who
immediately takes off his shoes & hangs them around his
neck. George Custer IV, third bachelor, weary from trying

to chew up a stork, takes out his harmonica & hands it to
first bachelor, Constantine, who after twisting it into form
of a fork, reaches into shoulder holster of the bodyguard,
removes a sickle, & replaces it with this out of shape musical
instrument . . . Luther begins to whistle "Comin thru the
Rye" George IV gives out with a wee chuckle . . . all
three continue down the avenue & dump the leftover fish
into the unemployment office. all except of course for a few
trout, which they give to the lady at the lost & found/ acci-
dent is reported at 3 P.M. it is ten below zero

do people tell you to your
face youve changed? do you
feel offended? are you seeking
companionship? are you plump?
4 ft. 5? if you fit & are
a full blooded alcoholic
catholic, please call
UH2-6969
                    ask for Oompa

Prelude to the Flatpick

mama/ tho i make no attempt to disqualify the somber
moody you. mama with the woeful shepherd on your shoul-
der. the twenty cent diamond on your finger. i play no
more with my soul like a tinker toy/ i now have the eyes of
a camel & sleep on a hook . . . to glorify your trials would
be most easy but you are not the queen—the sound is queen/
you are the princess . . . & i have been your honeyed
ground. you have been my guest & i shall not smite you

    "are there any questions?" the
    instructor asks. a blond haired
    little boy in the first row
    raises his hands an asks
    "how far to mexico?"

poor optical muse known as uncle & carrying a chunk of
wind & trees from the meadow & the kind of uncle that says
"holy moly" in a mild whisper meeting the farmer who say
"here. have some hunger for you." & lay some good fine
work in his nauseous lap/ chamber of commerce tries to tell
poor muse that minnesota fats was from Kansas & not so
fat, just notoriously heavy but theyre putting up super-

market across the meadow & that should take care of the
farmer

"does anybody wanna be anything
out of the ordinary?" asks the
instructor. the smartest kid
in class, who comes to school
drunk, raises his hand & says
"yes, sir. i'd like to be a
dollar sir"

the dada weatherman comes out of the library after being
beaten up by a bunch of hoods inside/ he opens up the
mailbox, climbs in & goes to sleep/ the hoods come out/ tho
they dont know it, theyve been infiltrated by a bunch of
religious fanatics . . . the whole group looks around for
some easy prey . . . & settle for some out of work movie
usher, who is wearing a blanket & a pilot's cap/ it is one
second to fourth of july & he does not fight back/ the dada
weatherman gets mailed to Monaco. grace kelly has another
kid & all the hoods turn into drunken business men

"who can tell me the name of
the third president of the

united states?" a girl with
her back full of ink raises
her hand & says "ernest tubb"

⁄more blue pills father & gobble the little quaint pills/ these
gushing swans, rituals & chickens in your sleep—theyve been
given the ok & the mad search warrant yes & you, the
famous Viking, snatching the time bomb from Sophia's
filter tip, down some jack daniels & get out there to meet
James Cagney . . . a swinging armadillo for your friend,
your faithful mob & mona lisa behind you . . . God ma,
the swains are baking him & how i wish i could ease him
& honor him with peace thru his veins. make him calm.
almighty & slay the horrible hippopotamus of his nitemare
. . . but i can take no martyr's name nor sleep myself in
any gust of dungeon & am sick with cavity . . . ludicrous,
the dead angel, monopolizing my vocal cords, gathering
her parent sheep onward & homeward into obituary. she's
hostile. she's ancient . . . aretha—golden sweet/ whose
nakedness is a piercing thing—she's like a vine/ your lucky
tongue shall not decay me

"is there anyone in class who
can tell me the exact hour his
or her father isnt home?" asks

the instructor. everybody
suddenly drops their pencils
& runs out the door—all excpt
of course the boy in the last
row wearing glasses & who's
carrying an apple

juicy roses to coughing hands assembling & pluck national
anthems! all hail! the football field ablaze with doves &
alleyways where hitchhikers wandering & setting fire to
their pockets resounding with the nuns & tramps & discard-
ing the weedy Syrian, surfs of halfreason, the jack & jills &
wax Michael from the church acre, who cry in their prime
& gag of their twins . . . empty ships on the desert &
traffic cops on the broomstick & weeping & hanging onto a
goofy sledgehammer & all the trombones coming apart, the
xylophones cracking & flute players losing their intimates
. . . as the whole band groaning throwing away measures
& heartbeats while it pays to know who your friends are
but it also pays to know you aint got any friends . . . like
it pays to know what your friends aint got—it's friendlier
to got what you pay for

down with you sam. down with your
answers too. hitler did not change

history. hitler WAS history/ sure
you can teach people to be beautiful,
but dont you know that there's a
greater force than you that teaches
them to be gullible—yeah it's called
the problem force/ they assign every-
body problems/ your problem is that you
wanna better word for world . . .
you cannot kill what lives an expct no-
body to take notice. history is alive/
it breathes/ now cut out that jive/
go count your fish. gotta go. someone's
coming to tame my shrew. hope they re-
moved your lung successfully. say hi
to your sister

                  love,
                  Wimp, Your
                  Friendly Pirate

Maria on a Floating Barge

in a sunburned land winter sleeps with a snowy head at the
west of the bed/Madonna. Mary of the Temple. Jane Rus-
sell. Angelina the Whore. all these women, their tears could
make oceans/ in a deserted refrigerator carton, little boys
on ash wednesday make ready for war & for genius . . .
whereas the weary archaic gypsy—yawning—warbles a
belch & tracking the cats & withstanding a ratsized cock-
roach she hardly appears & looks down upon her sensual
arena

    dear fang, how goes it old buddy?
    long time. no see. guess what? was
    gonna vote for goldwater cause you
    know, he was the underdog but then
    i found out about this jenkins thing,
    & i figger it aint much, but it's
    the only thing he does have going
    for him so i'm changing my vote to
    johnson. did you get the clothes i
    sent you? the shirt used to belong
    to sammy snead so better take good care
    of it

                     see you
                     Mouse

Sand in the Mouth of the Movie Star

a strange man we're calling Simply That wakes up to find "what" scribbled in his garden. he washes himself with a scrambled egg, puts his glasses in his pants & pulls up his trousers. there's a census taker knocking on his door & his orders for the day are nailed up on his mailbox reading that the route on junky monday is therefore as follows: two pints of soft liberty. a book of zulu sayings. citizen kane translated into dirty french. an orange t.v. studio. three bibles each autographed by the hillbilly singer who can sing salty dog the fastest. the back page of a 1941 daily worker. a salty dog. any daughter of any district judge. a tablespoon of coke & sugar heated to 300 degrees. jack london's left ear. seven pieces of deadly passport. a corn on the cob. five wooden pillows. one boy scout resembling charlie chan & a stolen titerope walker/ "what" is in my garden, he says over the phone to his friend, wally the fireman/ wally replies "i dont know. i really couldnt say. i'm not there" the man says "what do you mean, you dont know! what is written in my garden" wally says "what?" the man says "that's right" . . . wally replies that he is on his way down a pole & asks the man if he sees any relationship between doris day & tarzan? the man says "no, but i have some james baldwin & hemingway books" "not good enough" says wally, who again asks "what about a shrimp & an american flag? do you see any relationship between those two things?" the man says, "no, but i see bergman movies & i like stravinsky quite a lot" wally tries again & says "could you tell me in a million words what the bill of rights has to do with a feather?" the man thinks for a minute & says "no i cant do that but i'm a great fan of henry miller" wally slams the phone & the man, Simply That, he gets back into bed & begins reading "The Meaning of an Orange" in german . . . but by nitefall, he is bored. puts the book down & goes to shave while looking into a picture of thomas edison/ he decided over a bowl of milk to go out & have a good time & he opens the door & who's standing there but the census taker "i'm just a friend of the person who lives here" he says & goes back in the house & out the back door & down the street & into a bar with a moose head . . . the bartender gives him a double brandy, punches him in the groin & pushes him into a phone booth—obviously the man's crime is that he sees nothing resembling anything—he wipes the blood away from his groin with a hankie & decides to wait for a call/ "what" is still written in his garden. the clinics are integrated. the sun is still yellow. some people would say it's chicken . . . wally's going down a pole, the census taker arrives to make a phone call & phone booths dont have back doors/ junky monday driving, going down a one way street & turning into a friday the 13th . . . Ah wilderness! darkness! & Simply That

went five hours without a drink
of water. figger i'm ready for
the desert. wanna come? i'll
take along my dog. he's always
good for a laugh. pick yuh up
at seven

faithfully,
Pig

Roping Off the Madman's Corner

green maggie of profanity slapstick & her cast of seven coats
shining & fighting the milkmaids & high whining barndoor
slam—heavens! & righteous 38-20 slightly built on the ball
& chain & leashing the lawyer's pigeon while the rock n roll
lead guitar player does his mother's violets & his thing in the
middle of the bailiff's workbench & green maggie pushing
you into hotrod driver's eyes & he's lisping & he has no
money to pay for his language & maggie's not green & not
funny & life gets unbearable but the orator is not the re

porter & hanging around at the press room & shelling out to
the day crew & merchants of venice & why be bothered
with other people's set ups? it only leads to torture/ why
it's incredible! the world is mad with justice

dear mayor wagner. has anybody
ever told you, you look like
james arness? i am writing to
say that you are my son's idol.
could you please send your
schedule & repertoire to him, with
an autographed picture, at your
earliest convenience. he would
appreciate it kindly as that's
all he does is play your records
& defend you to his friends.
i do hope it's you that's reading
this & not some secretary
                        thank you
                        wishfully
                        Willy Purple

Saying Hello to Unpublished Maria

you taste like candy TUS HUESOS VIBRAN yowee &
i'm here because i'm starving & swallowing your tricks into
my stomach ERES COMO MAGIA like the greasy hotel
owner & it's not your father i'm hungry for! but i will bring
a box for him to play with. i am not a cannibal! dig your-
self! i am not a sky diver/ i carry no sticks of dynamite . . .
you say NO SERE TU NOVIA & i am not a pilgrim
neither TU CAMPESINA & you dont see ME crying over
that i cant be sad & wonderful & yippee TU FORMA EX-
TRANA your horseness amazes me/ i will stand—oh honor-
able—on the window of your countess even tho i am not a
window shade & bang SOLO SOY UN GUITARRISTA
all i do is drink & eat. all i have is yours

i'm telling you, the next time you
threaten to commit suicide in front
of me, i'm just gonna haul off an blow
your brains out y'hear! y'read me?
i'm so sick of having you bring me
down that i'd just as soon tie you
up & ship you off to red china.
another thing! you better take
good care of my mother. if i

hear that youre taking out your
misery on her, i'm coming to see
what i can do about things once &
for all . . . why dont you learn to
dance instead of looking for new
friends? dont you know that all
the friends have been taken

> yours,
> Hector Schmector

Forty Links of Chain (A Poem)

fox eyes from abilene—garbage poet from the
greyhound circuit & who has a feeling for the most lost
pieces of frost & boast of glass jaw & grampa
playing tiddlywinks & finks in the sinks & the barf &
gook in the book
of his cook, the ma & he's back in town
screwing around
with his hairlip down . . . he needs a dime &

writing rhyme You
dont have to guess . . . you know
the rest/ watch his nose! you can see where he goes
by offering to pay his dues—fox eyes, he's
got lotza blues—Tiny the chick with the wet news-
    paper,
she used to bring french fries to the mechanics &
whose right arm once went deaf & dumb
(it can happen to some)
she sees fox eyes come
climbing out of the stop sign & he's got a hangover
on top of it & she say "oh great grooby fox eyes. lead
    me to the
garbage" & he take her by the
lilywhitecottonpickin
hand & she say "yeah man i be a yellow monkey
    oowee!"
& he say "jus you folly me baby snooks! jus you folly
me & you feel fine!" & she say "giddy up & hi ho
silver &
i feel irish!" & both go off & get a bus schedule & she
saying all the time "steady big fella! steady!" while on
the other side of the street this mailman who looks like
shirley temple & who's carrying a lollypop stops &
looks at a cloud & just then the sky, he gets kinda
    pissed
& decides to throw his weight around a little & bloop a

tulip falls dead—the mailman starts talking to a park-
ing
meter & fox eyes, he say "it sure wasn't like this in
abilene" & it's a hurricane & a bus reading baltimore
leaves them in a total mess—she falls on her knees &
she say "i'm filthy" & fox eyes he say "go back to
florida baby there aint nothing here a city grill like
you can do" & the chick she does a handstand & she say
"i'm canadian!" & he say "get outa here & go to
florida!"
& she starts reciting fox eyes poems about salvation &
the
loony bin, strikes in the coloring book factory &
christmas
when they wrapped him in a shirt & he say "WHOA!
GET OUTA
HERE! I STEAL YO MONEY OWEE JESUS
GRILL! YOU SOME SLUMP!"
& she moans & groans & she say "oh i really do love
life &
love love & love living & he say "groovy! wail! wail!" &
she say "dont you understand" & she starts making
this terrible
scene right there in the middle of the street . . .
    Tiny—i met Tiny
later at an outrageous party—she was sitting under a
clock & i say

"you need an umbrella, friend" & she say "oh no! not
   another one!"
& she's got a new boyfriend now & he looks like
   machine gun kelly . . .
fox eyes—he lost all his money in a furnace—when last
   heard from
was riding fast freight out of salinas in a pile of lettuce &
still trying to collect unemployment . . . me? i made
   a special trip
downtown to get some graveyard figures—but it wasnt
   raining &
there were no buses going to baltimore/ just a broken
   jawed parking meter,
a water logged pen & a bunch of old shirley temple
   pictures
with her neck in a noose was all that i could find

look. i dont care if you are
a merchant marine. the next time
you start telling me i dont
walk right, i'm gonna get some
surfer to slap your face. i think
youre being very paranoid about
the whole thing . . . see you at the
wedding
                    stompingly yours
                    Lazy Henry

Mouthful of Loving Choke

crow jane from the wedding into the beast nest where wild
man peter the greek & ambassador frenchy do primitive
worship with hustling john from coney striking a pose &
dancing the pink velvet—all dramatics & curiously belong-
ing to the armenian hunchback resembling arthur murray
who's very turned off & gets syphilis & crow jane, she gets
the chilly blues watching but she speaks like a champion &
she dont kid around "what you gonna do? i mean besides
now's time for the good men promenade a party?" some
plaintive woos in the twilight & throats ripping & laughing
& fool's terror snapping like a tail & taking it in the ribs &
bop music where south walls quivering & colliding bosoms
& weigh the likes of maid marian's bandits & i repeat: two
face minny, the army derelict/ christine, who's hung up
on your forehead/ steve canyon jones who looks like mae
west in a closet/ screwy herman x, who looks like a closet/
jake the brown, who look like a forehead . . . dino, the
limping bartender, who steps in between Man Mountain
Sinatra who looks like the boy next door & Gorging
George, who has no last name . . . all these & their agents
& "how come you so smart crow jane?" & she say back
"how come you wanna talk so colored? & dont call me no
crow jane!" & superfreak pushing & shoving amazing—
totally amazing—"& i think i'm gonna do april or so is a
cruel month & how you like your blue eyed boy NOW

mr octopus?" when the four star colonels come in & every body says yankee doodle & plastered & some western union boy rides thru on a unicycle yelling "God save the secrets!" but is just coming on—he's mad & he's a horseshoe wizard—nobody cares tho & he's looking for the action & nobody cares about that either & he yells "help!" & two face minny, screaming, swinging from a chandelier & goes to bless him "you cant make nobody understand you too smart to think you know anything! not even john henry did that" crow jane jingle girl & she's a phantom & mouth like an oven & she dances on a cake of islam & "dont tell someone what you know they already know. that makes them think that you just like them & you aint!" . . . but then you take gwendeline, the different story & rides with lawrence of arabia & plays with her mercury—mumbling crummy world & "oh, the sadness!" . . . she gets some horny foreigners' attention but mainly all the cool people continue drawing noses on robert frost books "why be crazy on purpose?" say two face minny who's now on top the western union boy & steve canyon jones going off in the corner & crying "we aint never gonna get no messages that way!" . . . crow jane, she got this talent for robbing hardware stores & always being someplace at the wrong time but saying the right things "dont do your ideas—everybody's got those—let the ideas do you & talk with melody & money tempts ideas & it cant get close to melody & take all the money you can get but dont hurt nobody" crow jane, she got class "&

above all else, be all else!" oh the nites with broken arcs,
the backs of greensleeves & bruised film—homely & absurd
with rhythm & it gets to you after a while . . . a glass
sidewalk meeting the cracker boy's soul & trees like fire
hydrants standing in the path of the wooden horse & help
mama! help those that cannot understand not to understand
. . . the cracker boy wears spiked shoes but his hands are
bare/ peter & frenchy still dancing the cocktail tango—the
hunchback being carried out . . . honeymoon locked into
footsteps of the riderless stallion/ rome falling with driving
wishy washy half note—crawl with the blues feeling .   .
& the going daylight. crow jane say come, hang out her
limelight . . . there are green bullets in my throat/ i walk
sloppily on the sun feeling them turn into yellow keys—i
touch jane on the inside & i swallow

dear tom
have i ever told you that i
think your name ought to be
bill. it doesnt really matter
of course, but you know, i like
to be comfortable around people.
how is margy? or martha? or
whatever the hell her name is?
listen: when you arrive & you
hear somebody yelling "willy" it'll

be me that's who . . . so c'mon. there'll
be a car & a party waiting. it'll
be very easy to single me out, so
dont say you didnt know i was there
                              gratefully
                              truman peyote

The Horse Race

> ". . . always trying, always gaining"
>   —lyndon johnson

yes & so anyway on the seventh day, He created pogo, bat
masterson, & a rose colored diving board for His cronies/
the sky already strung up shivered like the top of a tent.
"what's all this commotion" he said to his main man, Gon-
zalas, who without batting an eyelash picked up a rake &
began flogging a cloud . . . seeing that Gonzalas had the

wrong idea, He told him to lay down the rake & go build
an ark/ when Gonzalas reaches twenty-five he starts won-
dering when his parents will kick off. it's nothing personal,
it's just that he needs some money & is beginning to resent
the fact that he hasnt been laid yet/ "why did you not
create an eighth day?" ask Gonzalas' chauffeur to his Sau-
sage Maker on the steps of the boom boom parlor/ while
handing in his perfume/ the sky, changing into a sexy
spaghetti odor, continues to tremble—Gonzalas, meanwhile,
sports a cane & tries to hide his korean accent/ edgar allan
poc steps out from behind a burning bush . . . He sees
edgar. He looks down & says "it's not your time yet" &
strikes him dead . . . Gonzalas enters/ places fifth in the
second

how come youre so afraid of
things that dont make any
sense to you? do people pass
you up on the street all the
time? do cars pass you up on
the highway? how come youre
so afraid of things that dont
make any sense to you? do you
water your raisins daily? do
you have any raisins? is there

anything that does make sense
to you? are you afraid of twelve
button suits? how come youre
so afraid to stop talking?
                    your valve cleaner
                    Tubba

Pocketful of Scoundrel

in a hilarious grave of fruit hides the wee gunfighter—a
warm bottle of roominghouse juice in the rim of his sheep-
skin/ lord thomas of the nightingales, bird of youth, ras-
putin the clod, galileo the regular guy & max, the novice
chess player/ the battles inside their souls & gloves being as
dead as their legends but only more work for the living
jesters—victims of assassination & dying comes easy . . .
on the other side of the tombstone, the amateur villain
sleeps with his tongue out & his head inside the pillow case/
nothing makes him seem different/ he goes unnoticed any-
way.

dear Sabu
it's my chick! she tells me that
she takes long walks in the woods.
the funny thing about it is that
i followed her one nite, & she's
telling me the truth. i try to
get her interested in things
like guns an football, but all
she does is close her eyes &
say "i dont believe this is happening"
last nite she tried to hang herself . . .
i immediately thought of having her
committed, but goddam she's my chick,
& everybody'd just look at me funny
for living with a crazy woman.
perhaps if i bought her her own car,
it would help/ can you fix it?
      thanx for listening
      All Petered Out

Mr. Useless Says Good-bye to Labor
& Cuts a Record

Phombus Pucker. with his big fat grin. his hole in the head.
his matter of fact knowledge of zen firecrackers. his little
white lies. his visions of sugar plums. his dishwater hands/
Phombus Tucker. with his bulldog wit. his theories on
atomic nipples. his beard & his backache/ Bombus Thucker.
with his soft boiled stovepipe. his aloneness & aloofness. his
hatred for crap/ Longus Bucker. with his numbers & deci-
mals. with his own special originality . . . spent hours &
hours carving his name in the sand. when all of a sudden,
a wave's commotion washed him & his name right into the
ocean (ho ho ho)

> look, you know i dont wanna
> come on ungrateful, but that
> warren report, you know as well
> as me, just didn't make it. you know.
> like they might as well have
> asked some banana salesman from
> des moines, who was up in toronto
> on the big day, if he saw anyone
> around looking suspicious/ or better

yet, they just coulda come & asked me
what i saw/ the doctors say i gotta tumor
coming up tho, so i got more important things
to do than to be bothered with straightening
out this whole mess . . . while youre down
there, see if you can get me murph the
surf's autograph

bye for now
your lightingman
Sledge

Advice to Tiger's Brother

you are in the rainstorm now where your cousins seek raw
glory near the bridge & the lumberjacks tell you of ex-
ploring the red sea . . . you fill your hat with rum & heave
it into the face of hailstone & not expect anything new to
be born . . . dogs wag their tails good-bye to you & robin
hood watches you from a stained glass window . . . the
opera singers will sing of YOUR forest & YOUR cities &

44

you shall stand alone but not make ceremony . . . an old
wrinkled prospector will appear & he will NOT say to you
"dont be possessive! dont wish to be remembered!" he will
just be looking for his geiger counter & his name wont be
Moses & dont count yourself lucky for not interfering—it
is petty . . . do not count yourself lucky

hi. just a note to say that ever
since the robbery, things've
kinda quiet down. altho theo's
kidnappers havent returned him
yet, dad got promoted to den
mother, so things are not all
going downhill/ mom joined the
future fathers of alaska. really
likes it/ you oughta see little
dumbbell. he's nearly two now.
talks like a fish & is already
starting to look like a cigar/
see you on your birthday
                    big brother
                    Dunk
p.s. adolph got you a trick piece of puke which
you put on the table & just watch the
girls throw up

On Watching the Riot from a Filthy Cell
or
(The Jailhouse Has No Kitchen)

standing on a bullet holed volkswagen, a bearded lepre-
chaun & he's wearing a topless mafia cape—holding up some
burning green stamps & he speaks out to the automobile
graveyard "four score & seven beers ago" & then he say
"etcetera" but his voice is drowned out by mickey mantle
hitting a grand slam . . . the mayor of the city, with alka
seltzer, climbs down from a limousine & asks "who the hell
is that leppo?" when a thousand angry tourists trample over
him all donning baseball gloves & here comes the squad/
"just who the hell are you?" speaks a garbage disposal "i'm
cole younger. gave my horse to the pony express. other'n
that, i'm just like you" a rousing cheer & the ball crashes
thru the fire box "i work for the city. before i swat you
you'd best tell me your occupation" "i'm an actor. tomor-
row & tomorrow & tomorrow lights this petty grace from
blow to blow like a poor stagehand pounding fury signi-
fying nothing. oh romeo, romeo, wherefor fart thou?
pretty good huh?" "i work for the city, i'll trample you
with my horse" "wanna hear some oedipus?" but beneath
the underground, Blind Andy Lemon & his friend, Lip,

sing rabbit foot blues in spurs & light pullover design by
Chung of paris—theyre standing in a fish bowl & every-
body's throwing marbles at them . . . outside, however,
after the tear gas disappears, we find that the leprechaun's
got his hand in a bandage & his beard's gone & the mayor,
we find out, is home making urgent phone calls to cardinal
spellman/ it has been a long time nite & everybody has had
lots of contact . . . i am ready for the cradle. the desert is
full of cattle

>   sorry for not writing sooner. had
> to have some teeth pulled. finally
> read the great glaspy. helluva book
> just a helluva one. that cat sure
> tells it like it is. not much happening
> around here. Chucky tried to get the
> donkey to jump a fence. you can guess
> what happened there. sis got married
> to a real dog. i punched him out
> right away. that's all for now
>   see yuh on thanxgiving
>   Corky

Hopeless & Maria Nowhere

raggity ann daughter of brazos & teeth in the necklace—
ornery in the flesh & the border with the big laugh of bull-
fight ghost & LIBERACION & she, with the leather mother
thief & peeking DOS PASOS MAS ee & crazy ALLA
LUEGO UN RAYO & insane DE SOL & taking the
brothers to bed & to boredom—heat in every corner like the
silent parrot by SALA UN DIA & mad like a hatter & the
pig barker—maria ESTAS DESNUDA she digs holes on my
eyes the size of the moon while her father, he keeps the hill
warm & uncritical from deacons & the youngster mission-
aries—maria sleep lightly PERO TE QUITARAS cursing
blond dynamite & TUS ROPAS . . . there is a hatchet in
maria's makeup & the spike driver moans, they sound on her
sink like the fornicating rattlesnake—friendly on her nature
& MARIA PORQUE LLORAS? & i give you my twelve
midnights & kick you with leapyear & protect you from the
crooked words & loyalty to the power works & these little
frogs with notebooks . . . maria PORQUE TU RIES?
freedom! she's the yardbird, the constant & the old lady is
made of marias & dogs yelping & RECUERDOS oh how the
furious yesterday, pyria SON HECHOS laying bang DE
ARCAICOS with simple simon NADAS is still right now
the poison nothing & maria, me & you, we make up three
TE QUIERO do not churchize my nakedness—i am naked

for you . . . maria, she says i'm a foreigner. she picks on
me. she pours salt on my love

      ok. so i shoot dope once in a
      while. big deal. what's it got
      to do with you? i'm telling you
      mervin, if you dont lay off me,
      i'm gonna rip you off some more
      where that scar is, y'hear? like
      i'm getting mad. next time you
      call me that name in a public
      cafeteria, i'm just gonna haul
      off & kick you so you'll feel
      it. like i aint even gonna get
      angry. i'm just gonna let one
      fly. fix you good
                    better watch it
                    The Law

A Confederate Poke into
King Arthur's Oakie

> ". . . later i left the Casino
> with one hundred & seventy
> gulden in my pocket. it's
> the absolute truth!"
> —fyodor dostoevsky

son of the vampire with his arm around betsy ross—he &
his society friends: Rain Man. Burt the Medicine. President
Plump. the Flower Lady & Baboon Boy . . . they all said
"happy new year, elmer & how's your wife, cecile?" & that
got them into the party free . . . once into the party, Burt
just stood around with a toothpick in the back of his neck
watching for the doctor & tho the card game was some-
thing else in itself, Flower Lady lost her shirt & went to
the bushes—who should come by but the little old wine
maker trying to be helpful—"get out of the picture" said
Flower Lady "you werent at the party!" . . . the little
old wine maker immediately took off his head & his belt &
who do you think it turned out to be but fabian—"i dont
care how many tricks you can do, just get outa here!" . . .
just then, this cable car on its way to washington came

rumbling down the hill carrying crossword puzzles for everybody—Rain Man yelled "watch out Flower Lady, there's an elephant coming!" but by this time she was singing auld lang syne with Baboon Boy, who'd snuck up, stuck a lead weight life jacket around fabian & threw him in the swimming pool—the Plump himself tried to give a warning but he was so drunk that he fell in a barrel & a tractor being driven by some dogs ran him over & dumped him into a garage . . . the world didnt stop for a second—it just blew up/ alfred hitchcock made the whole thing into a mystery & huntley & brinkley never slept for a week . . . the american flag turned green & andy clyde kept pestering about a back paycheck—every gymnasium in the world was picketed . . . son of the vampire, who got a divorce from betsy ross & now is with little red riding hood made it into january first carrying some empty stomachs—he & red, they got a job hiding door knobs & got paid good wages & like all people who decide not to go to any more parties, they put their money where their mouth is . . . & begin to eat it

translate this fact for me, dr.
blorgus: the fact is this: we
must be willing to die for
freedom (end of fact) now what
i wanna know about the fact is this: could

hitler have said it? de gaulle? pinocchio?
lincoln? agnes moorehead? goldwater? bluebeard?
the pirate? robert e. lee? eisenhower?
groucho smith? teddy kennedy? general franco?
custer? is it possible that jose melis
could have said it? perhaps donald o'connor?
i happen to be a library janitor, so could
you please clarify things a little for
me. thank you . . . by the way, if you do not
have a reply to me by this coming tuesday,
i will take it for granted that all these
forementioned people are all really the
same person . . . . see you later. have to take
down a picture of lady godiva as the
mental students are touring here in an
hour . . .

                    considerately yours,
                    Popeye Squirm

Guitars Kissing & the Contemporary Fix

along black winds & white fridays, they wash out water & shriek of jungle & lenny immune to the mathematics, he, the greasy quack—the vagabond god . . . he plants flowers in their saddle bags & speaks of Jesus brave & graduating—tragedy, the broken pride, shallow & no deeper than comedy—bites his path, his noise, his shadow . . . resign from mind the heart of light & approve the doom, the bending & the farce of happy ending . . . those that would gas the memory & shut out the might of right, the sight of those defending & offending the blossom girls of the dark, pregnant, permanent & pale outlaw . . . fair gloria the bowlegged singer, the sign painter's bastard—joanne, raped by the town historian & silver dolly, devirginated at 12, by her father, a miner—maybelle with a chopped up arm from an uncle—doublejointed barbara, who grinds a compact into the face of a druggist & maureen, the jealous lover . . . none of them raking leaves—ratting on friends who are telephone operators or paying for the like of an e.e. cummings . . . none of them falling for the "purr lost soul" talk of the hillbilly brawny gospel singer & lenny as the pilgrim angel—the crime but that he reigns in highway christ clothes, boots & a swagger . . the lone shark wolf in a world where piemen castrate the dogs & cities for Du Pont, cat magazines & hiding in machines they chew gum, their seeds, their por-

traits . . . lenny leaves the woodchuck, the veteran of
foreign war to his plymouth 6, his murder page—the Arms
Bros chair & to his kidnapper & the radio siren/ the com-
munists would call him lazy & the veteran calls him a bum
& yo ho ho & a bottle of rum but he's nice to priests & dont
tangle with the mayor's daughter 'n law . . . he wears silk
& bows to yoyos, barbells & the strangers—he steals bow ties
& heading for the north & waves to soldiers with amputated
hands who picked up broken ashtray pieces & staying clear
of muffled & exploding roosters, he pets ornaments & twin
pipes/ there is a rhapsody to his toughness & he sure is
warm & worthlessly wild

    the deer thru the woods quite out of it
    all shall never be the slave but the target
    for military & freedom's legs having no
    substitute for death when sunday professor & the
    children come out, say "watch it, you bound to
    stumble now!" & the lady in waiting just collapsing
    & asked if that's a threat or perhaps a friendly
    warming & the innocent coon being scraped on the
    table—liberty, an orphan sonnet, unwritten &
    having no eyes & needs, no defense & getting
    some glass in the veins—the conspiracy to kill
    the free & romantic to custom operating regularly
    on schedule & attacking now the once that run

with no sidecar . . . go ahead, shoot! all you need
is a license & a weak heart

thru the braided hair & loafing beer can beach of wood—
brains of the roadhouse & panel trucks filled with cucumber
funk, jim beam sweating & lords & ladies in the rear view
mirror—humanity in the gang bang mood & yodeling swim-
mers—the kinks from strike town & itty bitty pretty one
lapping up the crankcase rotgut & lenny laughing in a fake
sombrero & the jugglers trying to smother the queers & the
girls from big city & panoramic way, you found lenny,
the dog catcher killer & motorcycle saint—you either love
him or hate him—attracting the filthy mamas, Tom the
Wretched, Mike the Bull & Hazel, the pornographic back
slapper . . .lenny can take the bad out of you & leave you
all good & he can take the good out of you & leave you all
bad/ if you think youre smart & know things, lenny plays
with your head & he contradicts everything youve been
taught about people/ he is not in the history books & he
either makes you glad to be you or he makes you hate to
be you . . . you know he's some kind of robber yet you
trust him & you cannot ignore him

. . . the lion's den then, & anchors away & you remember
the table—the hopped up table of worldly wiggies & un-
patriotics & the slut madonna with her squatter's rights &

everybody sexy & picking on the car thieves & some bum-
bling sacred cow telling how he marched right in &
trimmed this chicken just like that but when peter pan of
the throttle bums gets up to go someplace, it's growling &
wondering & sentimental because you know he never does—
while gloria talks of the fish in her finger with her hair
dyed pink & speaking of tomorrow, calling it sunday & the
engine slams & really slams into first gear—& it sounds like
john lee hooker coming & oh Lordy louder like a train . . .
the punchdrunk sailor with a scar below his nose suddenly
slaps & kicks little sally & makes her let go of the bottoms
of his dungarees & you Know he knows something's hap-
pening & it aint the ordinary kind of sound that you can
see so clearly & carrrrrashhhhh & a technicolor passion of
berserk & napoleonic & suicide & lenny vanishes in the day-
time & a bridge girder all lonesome & gone & the trumpets
play what theyve always been taught to play in time of
emergency—Babylon's sweetheart & the redblooded boy
oozing all over & shock, the defunct rockabilly in a blind-
fold—dissolve into the motherland for touch & kneeling to
instinct, gypsies & into the most northernmost forest he can
find

. . . a roaring free for all is witnessed later between as fol-
lows: rabbit seller, who, because he lives in a room where
the rain continues to fall thru the chimney, always has a
chronic cough & is constantly in an al capone type mood-

call him White Man/ the ex faggot g.i., who now trans-
ports dummies from macy's to yankee stadium & whose
ears always bleed in heavy weather—call him Black Man/
the hatcheck girl with a glass eye, whose father taught her
how to walk exactly like P.T. Barnum & now she discovers
it means nothing—call her Audience/ the candle stick
maker, with a mouthful of plastic & his pockets full of used
matches—call him Reward/ the bathing beauty who wears
a turban full of meatballs—call her Success/ the tug of war
rope & a holy bell—boom & the pumphouse guardian step-
ping out of his coocoo & saying "words are objects! sight
is ego! did any of you freaks ever know a lenny? i can
remember his last name . . ." & then some vigilante, he
say "get back in your clock! you ever heard of lions one,
christians nothing?" & after sending hitler out to murder
the poor guardian, he jumps back into the christians &
clocks & all types of mink, milk & vitamin C—grannies in
titepants & barechested undertakers goosing preachers
wearing egg cartons & U.N. generals in bathrobes & their
feet stuck in bongo drums & three million jealous teachers
in used roy acuff strings all flunking little de gaulles &
prison choruses bursting & singing hallaluyah . . . every-
body even Good St. Doc & the bird scientist sucking
scruples & nipples & trying to hide their shit . . . everybody
saying "disaster!" & pointing & examining hanging clowns &
making reports & going "gah gah" at dead pontiacs & babies
in Lorca graves . . the tax collector stealing everybody's

useless sacrifice & H.G. Wells unheeded . . Lulu the
Smith having a heart attack at the birth of a black angel &
john brown, Luke the snob & Achilles all reaching for the
Flying Saucer . . . one day, the day of the Tambourines,
the astronaut, Micky McMicky, will remove a thumb from
his mouth—say "go to hell" while lenny i'm sure is already
in a resentful heaven

        dear dropout magazine,
        gentlemen:
        i understand that you are currently
        putting a book together about
        blacklisted or blackheaded artists or something.
        if it is the former, then i shall have to
        recommend that you place jerry lee lewis first
        an foremost. if it is the latter, then i shall
        have to recommend that you contact the american
        medical society to discover the exact worth of
        such an undertaking
                        in all respects, i remain
                        a rabble rouser from the mountains
                        Zeke the Cork

Advice to Hobo's Model

paint your shoes delilah—ye walk on white snow where a
nosebleed would-disturb the universe . . . down these nar-
row alleys of owls an flamenco guitar players, jack paar
an other sex symbols are your prizes—check into the bath-
rooms where bird lives for when he comes flying out with
a saber in his wing—a country music singer by his side—
digesting a carrier pigeon . . . ye just might change your
style of fornicating, sword swallowing—ye just might
change your way of sleeping on nails—paint your shoes the
color of the ghost mule—the paper tiger's teeth are made of
aluminum—youve a long time to Babylon—paint your shoes,
delilah—paint them with a sponge

look! like i told you before, it doesnt
matter where it's at! there's no such
thing. it's where it's not at that you
gotta know. so what if tony married his
mother! what's it got to do with your life?
i really have no idea why youre so unhappy.
perhaps you ought to change your line of
work. you know. like how long can someone
of your caliber continue to paint pencil

sharpeners . . . see you next summer, good to
know youre off the wagon.

prematurely yours,
Funka

A Blast of Loser Take Nothing

jack of spades—vivaldi of the coin laundry—wearing a hip-
ster's dictionary—we see him brownnosing around the
blackbelts & horny racing car drivers—dashing to & fro like
a frightened uncle remus . . . on days that he gets no mail
he rises early, sticks paper up the pay phones & cons the
bubble gum machines . . . "the world owes me a living"
he says to his half-hawaiian cousin, the half-wit, joe the
head who is also planning to marry a folksinger next
month—"round & round, old joe clark" is being recited
from the steps of the water & light building as jack ambles
by with a case full of plastic bubbles—things look well for
him: he can imitate cary grant pretty good. he knows all

the facts why mabel from utah walked out on horace, the lightingman from Theatre Altitude. he has even stumbled onto a few hairy secrets of mrs. Cunk, who sells fake blisters at the world's fair—plus being able to play a few foreign legion songs on the yoyo & always managing to look like a grapefruit in case of emergency . . . he brags about his collection of bruises & corks & the fact that he pays no attention to the business world. he would rather show his fear of the bomb & say what have you done for freedom than to praise an escaped mental patient who pisses on the floor of junior's delicatessen—jack of spades, with his axe, the record player. with his companion, the menu. & his destination, a piece of kleenex—never touches the cracks on the sidewalk—"jack" says his other cousin, Bode-guard, half danish & half surfer, "how come you always act like Crazy, jackie gleason's friend? i mean wow! aint there enough sadness in the world?" jack walks by in a flash—he wears ear plugs—from the steps of the water & light building, the band, after knocking all the juice out of their horns, begin to play on my papa . . . jack, shocked, takes a second look, raises his hand in a nazi salute. a woods-man, walking by with an axe, drops it. a D.A.R. woman flies off the handle. looks at jack. says "in some places, you'd be arrested for obscenity" she doesnt even hear the band . . . she falls down a sidewalk crack/ the band leader, paying no attention, does a slight curtsy, sneezes. points his wand at the classical guitar . . . a street cleaner

bumps into jack & says & i quote "o.k. so i bumped into
you. i dont even care. i got me a little woman at home. i
know a good radiator down the block. man, i aint never
gonna starve. would you like to buy a pail?" jack, amazed,
rearranges his collar & heads off to the bell telephone hour.
which is located beyond the next cop car . . . he passes
a hot dog stand. a sauerkraut hits him in the face . . . the
band is playing malaguena salerosa—the D.A.R. woman
pops out of the sidewalk, hears the band, screams, starts
doing the jerk. the street cleaner steps on her . . . jack
hasnt eaten all day. his mouth tastes funny—he has his un-
published novel in his hand—he wants to be a star—but he
gets arrested anyway

hi y'all. not much new happening.
sang at the vegetarian convention
my new song against meat. everybody
dug it except for the plumbers neath
the stage. this one little girl,
fresh out of college & i believe
president of the Dont Stomp Out the
Cows division of the society. she tried
to push me into one of the plumbers.
starts a little chaos going, but you
know me, i didnt go for that not one
little bit. i say "look baby, i'll sing

for you & all that, but just you dont
go pushing me, y'hear?" i understand
that theyre not gonna invite me back
cause they didnt like the way i came on
to the master of ceremony's old lady, all
in all, i'm making it tho. got a new song
against cigarette lighters. this matchbook
company offered me free matches for the rest
of my life, plus my picture on all the
matchbooks, but you know me, it'd take a
helluva lot more'n that before i'd sell out—
see you around nomination time

your fellow rebel
kid tiger

making love on maria's friend

yawn to foxy queenie school teacher—gone, decatur &
entering the pink highway—your black mongrel vagabond,
your rat from Delphi—now he shall tattle on your nauseous

bra—your hair in chains & speak TU CAMINO while your
El Paso ideals, they celebrate ES TERCIOPELO they leave
your gruesome body—your structure falling, you listen for
a lazy siren & some young Spaniard to buy your wounds,
your pregnant drawl . . . yawn to queenie of the Goya
painting seeking poor Homer QUEDATE CONMIGO
while the dikes break & count your number & Baby Mean
crying NO PREDENDAS while author Fritz from your
industrial south yelling what's this all about & get the hell
home, queenie & you, queenie, the spider—the sweat web's
got you—you beg your arms to move—you pray to be
righteous—you look for postcards & teddy bears for pay-
offs—the partisans, they laugh CON TUS PIERNAS &
the boys with brown rags, they whisper of the bust &
already they have Leo the Sneak & Doc's gonna have to
leave by noon—St. Willy hides in the pawnshop PARA
QUEENIE you need not fear & nobody's chasing—you
want to be held LA ERRONEA DAMA & dig into your
purse—forget your pupils & pay for your partner & bother-
ation—the shadow of your boss, it is your felony—author
Fritz would like to suck your toe—your holiday be gone
soon & vanishing like your life LA CHOTA the grass cuts
your feet & Socrates' Prison is your goal AHI VIENEN
you are the wrong lady—you threaten nobody—spend your
money on health food & you shall be run over by a truck—
they'll put a tag on you—send you home to Fritz—Fritz will
cry for a week & marry your nurse—the dikes will curl

their mouths but you'll still be the wrong one TODOS
SON DE LA CHOTA live now . . . live before you
board your Titanic--reach out, Queenie, reach out—feel for
equal saggy skin & believe this dark playboy licking ink
from your notebook—see the cages & screaming ghosts &
you with the gall to think that ruins are buildings . . .
take your bloody glands & medallion & make love once
freely—it means nothing so wear a top hat—travel on a slow
ship back to your guilt, your pollution, the kingdom of
your blues

hi. watcha doing? how's the new religion?
feel any different? gave it up myself. just
couldnt make all the auctions and frankly,
i's running out of bread. you know how it
is, like about that little old lady in the
back building all the time pointing telling
me that God is watching. you know, like for a
while there, i's scared to take a shit. anxious
to get together with you. i know you dont wear
bow ties anymore but i'm interested in other
aspects of your new faith too. by the way, are
you still in the keyhole business? cant wait
to talk to you

bye,
your buddy,
Testy

Note to the Errand Boy
as a Young Army Deserter

wonder why granpa just sits there & watches yogi bear?
wonder why he just sits there & dont laugh? think about it
kid, but dont ask your mother. wonder why elvis presley
only smiles with his top lip? think about it kid, but dont
ask your surgeon. wonder why the postman with one leg
shorter'n the other kicked your dog so hard? think about
it kid, but dont ask any mailman. wonder who ronald
reagan talked to about the foreign situation? think about
it kid, but dont ask any foreigners. wonder why the me-
chanic, whose wife shot herself with a gun she got from
his best friend, hates castro so much? wonder why castro
hates rock n roll? think about it kid, but dont ask no roll.
wonder how much the man who wrote white christmas
made? think about it, but dont ask no made. wonder what
bobby kennedy's really got against jimmy hoffa? think
about it, but dont ask no bobby. wonder why frankie shot
johnny? go ahead, wonder, but dont ask your neighbor
. . . wonder who the carpet baggers are? think, but dont
ask no carpet. wonder why youre always wearing your
brother's clothes? think about it kid, but dont ask your
father. wonder why general electric says that the most im-
portant thing for a family to do is stick together? think
about it kid, but dont ask no together . . . wonder what

paydirt is? go ahead, wonder . . . wonder why the other
boys wanna beat you up so bad? think about it kid, but
dont ask nobody

       yes. ok. i guess youre a pumpkin.
       yes, it's true i referred to you as "that
       chinese girl" you have a right to
       be angry. but what i want to know
       is just what have you got against
       the chinese anyway?
                       maybe we can still work
                       it out
                       properly yours,
                       prince goulash

Taste of Shotgun

the roar of our engines promises us cover—we wear choking
pants & are slaves to appetite—we get stoned on joan craw-

ford & form teeming colonies & die of masculine conversa-
tion . . . Marcellus, wearing khaki when madness struck
him, immediately filed suit against an illegitimate son be-
longing to someone else—Josie said everybody at the trial
came with a blowgun . . . Tom Tom made Melodius hate
him, then jumped from a window—we are all alike & place
scorpions neatly in our insides—we take pills thru the ass—
we praise faggot missionaries & throw homosexuals into
phenomenon gutters . . . in the winter a blackface musi-
cian announces he is from Two Women—he spends his free
time trying to peel the moon & he's here to collect his
eight cent stamp—Marguerita the pusher, wheeling a cartful
of Thursday up Damaen's Row yelling "cockles & mus-
cles," kills him for getting in the way of her appetite . . .
the rewards are few on Chemical Isle—little girls hide per-
fume up their shrimps & there are no giants—the warmon-
gers have stolen all our german measles & are giving them
to the doctors to use as bribes—i stayed awake for three
hours last nite with Pearl—she claimed to have walked by
a rooming house i once lived in—we had nothing in com-
mon, me & Pearl—i shared her boredom & had nothing to
give her—i was drunk & entertained myself . . . we wish
to make journeys & use everything except our feet & we
meet tongue tied broken vulgar geeks with gorilla hand-
shakes & drunken Hercules waits for us on our beds & we
must salute him & he says that the new helicopters have
arrived & "this is your geek" & "you will take your orders

from him" yes the rewards are few here but there are no
oaths to take nor mental strokes—excpt for the self con-
scious insanity brought in by hunters with radios wearing
religious clothes, all goes well . . . Angola being bombed
this morning, i right now am happy with nausea—my head
is suffocating—i am gazing into the big dipper with silver
buttoned blouse in my nostrils—i'm glad Marguerita's all
right—i Do feel expensive

> i am leaving my kid on your
> doorstep, if youre so hot, you'll
> see that he gets taken care of.
> after all, he's your kid too. i
> expct to see him in about twenty
> years, so you better do a good
> job. i am going into the mountains
> to find work. i am taking along
> the food. remember luv, keep the
> stove clean & watch the gas tank
> yours
> louie louie

Mae West Stomp (A Fable)

train goes by every nite the same old time & he, same old
man, sits looking into a rosary which reads "i told you so"
while rocking back & forth thinking about his eldest son,
Hambone, who's in jail for life—buying beer for the kids &
murdering the grocer with a pocket comb—this same old
man, with nothing but a bathtub full of memories consist-
ing of: a few Baby Huey for President buttons—a deck of
cards with the aces missing—some empty deodorant bottle
—a pamphlet of egyptian slogans—three pant legs that dont
match & a hollow lynch rope . . . sits in a candy wrapper
chair muttering day in court—day in court—i'll get it yet—
my day in court—a dapper young gentleman with chapped
lips rubbed them on the old man's neck today—the little old
man is planning revenge just as the same old time train
shakes his whistler's mother painting off the wall & it gooses
him to . . . day in court—i'll get it yet—yesterday was not
so good either—a fox left him in a clump of mud & some
little pest let him have it right in the kisser with a mixture
of bamboo, barley & rotten ice cream—there he sits wishing
he could get thru to the president—the little old man's
bowels ache so he opens the window to breathe some good
fresh air—he inhales deeply—there is a line full of wet under-
wear—used tires dirty bed sheets—hats—chicken feathers—
an old watermelon—paper plates & some other garments—

johnny drumming wind—an indian, passing thru on his way
to st. louis, is standing neath the old man's window—"amaz-
ing" he says as he looks up & sees all this stuff on the clothes-
line suddenly get sucked into a hole . . . next day, the rent
collector comes to get the rent—finds that the old man has
disappeared & that the room's full of garbage—the lady who
owns the clothesline, she reports theft to the robbery de-
partment—"all my valuables have been stolen"—she mutters
to the inspector—the train still goes by at the same old time
& johnny drumming wind, he gets picked up for vagrancy
—the rent collector looks around—steals a broken coocoo
"i think i'll give it to my wife" he says—his wife, who is six
feet tall & wears a fez, & who, at the minute, by weird cir-
cumstance, is riding by on that same old time train—all in
all, not much happens in chicago

　　　i'm not saying that books are
　　　good or bad, but i dont think
　　　youve ever had the chance to find
　　　out for yourself what theyre all
　　　about—ok, so you used to get B's
　　　in the ivanhoe tests & A minuses
　　　in the silas marners . . . then you
　　　wonder why you flunked the hamlet
　　　exams—yeah well that's because one
　　　hoe & one lass do not make a spear—

the same way two wrongs do not make
a throng—now that youve been thru
life, why dont you try again . . . you
could start with a telephone book—
wonder woman—or perhaps catcher in
the rye—theyre all the same & everybody
has their hat on backwards thru the
stories

                     see you at the docks
                     helpfully yours,
                     Sir Cringe

Black Nite Crash

aretha in the blues dunes—Pluto with the high crack laugh
& rambling aretha—a menace to president as he was jokingly
called—go—yea! & the seniority complex disowning you
. . . Lear looking in the window dangerous & dragging a
mountain & you say "no i am a mute" & he says "no no i've
told the others you were Charlie Chaplin & now you must

live up to it—you must!" & aretha saying "split Lear—none
of us got the guts for infinity—take your driving wheel &
split . . . & aretha next—she's got these hundred Angel
Strangers all passing thru saying "i will be your Shakti &
your outlaw kid—pick me—pick me please—ah c'mon pick
me" & aretha faking her intestinal black soul across all the
fertile bubbles & whims & flashy winos—Jinx, Poet Void &
Scary Plop all skipping to hell with their bunnies where
food is cheaper & warmer & Nucleur Beethoven screaming
"oh aretha—i shall be your voodoo doll—prick me—let's
make somebody hurt—draw on me whoever you wish! ah
pretty please! my bastard frame—my slimy self—penetrate
unto me—unto me!" Scholar, his body held together by
chiclets—raw beans & slaves of days gone by—he storms in
from the road—his pipe nearly eaten "look! she burps of
reality" & but he's not even talking to anybody—a moth
flies out of his pocket & Void, the incredible fall apart re-
minds you once more of america with the dotted line—use-
less motive—the moral come on & silver haired men hiding
in the violin cases . . . on a mound of phosphorus & suc-
cess stands the voluptuous coyote eagle—he holds a half
dollar—an anchor sways across his shoulders "good!" says
Nucleur Beethoven "good to see there are some real birds
around" "that's no bird—that's just a thief—he's building an
outhouse out of stolen lettuce!" signs aretha—Sound of
Sound—who really doesnt give a damn about real birds or
outhouses or any Nucleur Beethoven—approval, complaints

& explanations—they all frighten her—she has no flaws in her
trumpet—she knows that the sun is not a piece of her

    the audio repairman stumbles
    thru the door with "sound is sacred—
    so come in & talk to us" written on
    the back of his shirt

Hostile Black Nite Crash

on this abandoned roof or pagoda stool they place you &
you hear voices saying things like "titen 'm up Joe—keep 'm
titened up" & then Orion looking evil & he wipes you off &
keeps you clean & Familiar Face himself "i heard you been
eating some eggs? any truth to that?" & Orion licking his
flesh & trouble in mind blues & shades of fire hydrants . . .
YOU—the fire hydrant & Beau Geste, a fire hydrant—fail-
ures completely & walking to Gibraltar & trying to find
your energy—get your kicks & shadow box your language

. . . Faust from the garden—Emancipation Anne, who
looks like a hungarian deer & Chump with a brain like an
iceberg all imitating Africa . . . Dead Lover who hitchhikes
& brags & says he's going to Carthage & he keeps repeat-
ing "when i die" but then his mind goes black & blue &
methodist butter erupting & Twinkle Clown with arabic
lettering on his forehead wanting everybody to experience
his fright "you must experience my fright to be my friend!"
so says he to Lucy Tunia, whose vegetarian legs shine like
mahogany & who comforts Twinkle Clown in his fits when
he has no harem . . . Zing & Orion stutters & coughs &
SHAZAMMM—the opium ghost neath the ferris wheel—
on the side of the highway—where nobody can stop—where
he can cause no trouble—where the show must go on . . .
this is where He wishes to die—He wishes to die in the
midst of cathedral bells—He wishes to die when the torna-
does strike the roofs & stools "so much for death" he will
say when he dies

the newsboy comes in the back door—
his big toe sticks thru his shoe—he
carries a piece of peeling with a
number on it—he makes a phone call—
then he blows his nose

Unresponsible Black Nite Crash

the united states is Not soundproof—you might think that
nothing can reach those tens of thousands living behind the
wall of dollar—but your fear Can bring in the truth . . .
picture of dirt farmer—long johns—coonskin cap—strangling
himself on his shoe—his wife, tripping over the skulls—her
hair in rats—their kid is wearing a scorpion—the scorpion
wears glasses—the kid, he's drinking gin—everybody has bal-
loons stuck into their eyes—that they will never get a sun-
tan in mexico is obvious—send your dollar today—bend over
backwards . . . or shut your mouths forever

　　the bully comes in—kicks the newsboy
　　you know where—& begins ripping away
　　at the audio repairman's shirt

Electric Black Nite Crash

nature has made the young West Virginia miners not want to be miners but rather get this '46 Chevy—no money down —take to Geneva . . . hunting for the likes of escape & Lord Buckley & Sherlock Holmes about to be his mother turning to Starhole the Biology Amazon saying "i dont want to be my mother!" & e.e. cummings—spell it right—wrapping his leftover chicken bones in a pig tail belonging to Bronx Baby No. 2 & she thinks the world's coming to an end & tries to organize a rally & her 320 pound Frenchman who sticks his tongue out at her father—he dont want no part of it—"i dont wanna go to no San Quentin! i'm not a criminal—i'm a foreigner & i cant help it if you dig e.e. cummings but me—like ah said—i'm just a foreigner" & she throws all these leftover chicken bones into his face & some celebrities passing by—they witness the whole thing & take down the serial numbers . . . Mona carries a lone ranger advertisement on her left front breast—Mona's cousin—this 320 pound Frenchman—he resembles Arthur Conan Doyle . . . Mona—she resembles a sexy Buddha & always looks like she's standing over the Golden Gate . . . she dont dig e.e. cummings—she digs Fernando Lamas—i am on a black train going west—there is no aretha on the desert—just—if you want—memories of aretha—but aretha teaches not to depend on memory—there is no aretha on the desert

the stripper comes in wearing an
engagement ring—she asks for lemonade,
but says she'll settle for a sandwich—
the newsboy grabs her—yells "lord have
mercy"

Somebody's Black Nite Crash

from entire Mexico & gay innocence once comes Satan of
Autumn—from the gentleness & barbarian bebop & lone-
some rooms where you must put a nickel in the parking
meter—into the arms of notorious daughters—daughters who
get social poems published in bazaar & fashion magazines &
wonder of adventure—beer barrel polkas & cat goofballs
"why didnt HUAC get custer?" say some "how did robert
burns escape hitler is what i'd like to know!" say the smarter
ones—all the hipster T-bone heads & wheel chair Marxists
wishing to be in Kansas City '51 & Satan of Autumn & his
friend, I DONT KNOW YOU, gnawing farts in the farm-
lands & coming back & telling everybody & then I DONT

KNOW YOU finally coming to the conclusion "what good's it all to tell everybody about anything—they all got alibis?" & then Montana coming & Aztec Landlords themselves—their atomic fag bars being looted & Bishops disguised as chocolate prisoners & the empty Barbary Coast haunted houses where the bureaucrats—the dreamy Huxley hanger oners—the New Awake with money & no place else to go & the ex cop who writes verse & thinks of himself as a salami & Gabby—the crippled horror from Telegraph Avenue but who wants to hear of this—who really wants to hear of this? "who wants to hear anything? we just a part of a generation! just one mangy grubby part!" said I DONT KNOW YOU one day to Satan & it was autumn "you mean like the hula hoop happening?" "no—like the crucifixion happening!" "like the Modern beat?" "like the beat of a peach tree" . . . both Satan & I DONT KNOW YOU—they skip thru the New York race track—all the typical renaissances & a blond that looks like ezra pound & they go right into Summer—without winter—seeing them so unsuffered, Lu with a crew cut, one of the chicks that write the big fat writings—her mouth hangs open—some beggar comes out of his hovel & hangs a hair from her lip—a streetcar crashes . . . but all in all—nobody really cares

the chamber of commerce all come in—
each member carrying hand grenades—

everything turns into blood—excpt for
the jukebox, a stranger wearing a——
calendar, & a postcard of a greek
building . . . which the owner of the
place has left on top of the radiator
by mistake/ the play now begins . . . it
is all in the past . . . i will not be
so insulting as to write it for you

Seems Like a Black Nite Crash

between the shrieking mattress in the kitchen & Time, a mysterious weekly—Tao—a fingertip on his chin, his knees knocking together—Tao—he shows the inside of his mouth to a column of faces "does this mean you must take a nap today?" & Phil Silvers eating a banana—he is inside of the column of faces—Tao is quiet & Phil pokes Duff the Hero —a miser from the Aegean Sea—a vast desert in his head—he has plenty of self confidence & lets yokels test bombs in his brain—"love is a ghost thing" says Duff "it goes right thru you" Tao strains—he looks almost pornographic "some tonsils!" says Phil, who now wears long suspenders & tells Duff to keep up the self confidence "self confidence is deceiving" says Mr. O'toole—a husband of questionable virtue "it gives people without balls a sense of virility" "does your wife own a cow?" says Phil, who has now turned into an inexpensive Protestant ambassador from Nebraska & who speaks with a marvelous accent "what do you mean does my wife own a cow?" "are you from Chicago then?" asks the ambassador . . . Tao's face—meanwhile—becomes so big— it disappears "where'd he go?" says Duff—who's not so much of a hero anymore but rather a jolly youth that hates degenerates & is supposed to be in school anyway . . . Mr. O'toole—falls out of his chair "i must find some railroad tracks—i must put my ear to the tracks—i must listen for a train"—the column of faces—all together now—a munching chorus "DONT GET KILLED NOW"—repeat—"dont get killed now" . . . yes & between this mattress shrieking & that mysterious weekly lay the slave counties—Doris Day gone & Pacific fog—a Studebaker in twilight—crash—& breaking down the honkytonk doors & strange left handed moonmen—from Arkansas & Texas & vagabonds with girlie magazines from Reed College—cellars & Queens—they all shouting "watch me Tao—watch me—i'm high—watch me now!" . . . that lonesome feeling—paralyzing—that lonesome feeling—or aretha—my mama didnt raise no fool—i have nothing new to add to that feeling . . . slide on vomit

—better'n working with a shovel—Reject—God Bless Holy
Phantomism & damn the farewell parties—statistic books—
the politicians   . . the column of faces—all together now
—raising the flag & staring up to a hole in it—chanting "it's
halloween! can Tao come out & play?"—getting no reaction
& shouting louder—all in unison now—"IT'S HALLOW-
EEN . . . CAN TAO COME OUT & PLAY?"

  give up—give up—the ship is lost: go
  back to san bernardino—stop trying to
  organize the crew—it's every man for
  himself—are you a man or a self? when
  the coast guard gets there, stand up
  proudly & point—dont be a hero—everybody's
  a hero—be different—dont be a conformist—
  forget about all those sea shanties—just
  stand up & say "san bernardino" in a deep
  monotone . . . everybody will get the message
        your benefactor
        Smoky Horny

Chug A Lug—Chug A Lug
Hear Me Hollar Hi Dee Ho

he was propped in the crutch of an oak tree—looking down
—singing "there's a man going round taking names" indeed
—i nod howdy—he nods howdy back "well he took my
mother's name—lef' me there in pain" i, who am holding a
glass of sand in one hand & a calf's head in the other—i look
up & say "are you hungry?" & he say "there's a man going
round taking names" & i say "good nuff" & keep walking—
his voice rings thru the valley—it sounds like a telephone—
it is very disturbing—"you need anything up there?"—i'm
going to town" he shakes his head "well he took my sister's
name & i aint never been the same" "right-o" i say—tie my
shoelace & keep walking—then i turn & say "if you need
any help getting down, just you come to town & tell me" he
doesnt even hear—"well he took my uncle's name & you
know he wasnt to blame" "groovy" i say & continue my
way to town . . . it couldnt've been more'n a few hours
later when i happened to be passing by again—in the spot
where the tree was, a lightbulb factory now stood—"did
there used to be a guy here in a tree?" i yelled up to one of
the windows—"are you looking for work?" was the reply
. . . it was then when i decided that marxism did not have
all the answers

why are you so frightened of
being embarrassed? you spend a lot of
time on the toilet dont you? why
dont you admit it? why are you so
embarrassed to be frightened?

your uncle
Matilda

Paradise, Skid Row & Maria Briefly

fatty Aphrodite's mama—i bend to you . . . & with sex
mad eternity at my vegetable shadow—i, wiping my hands
on the horse's neck—the horse burping & you of the Indiana
older brother—he who whips you with his belt & you who
does not look for reason to your torture & i want your hori-
zontal tongue—within Reflex—the perfect doom & these
cruel nitemares where brickmasons introduce me to hideous
connections & Marx Brothers grunting NO QUIERO TU
SABIDURIA & your thighs be half awake & me so Sick so
Sick of these lovers in Biblical roles—"so youre out to save

the world are you? you impostor—you freak! youre a con-
tradiction! youre afraid to admit youre a contradiction!
youre misleading! you have big feet & you will step on
yourself all the people you mislead will pick you up! you
have no answers! you have just found a way to pass your
time! without this thing, you would shrivel up & be nothing
—you are afraid of being nothing—you are caught up in it
—it's got you!" i am so Sick of Biblical people—they are
like castor oil—like rabies & now i wish for Your eyes—you
who does not talk any business & supplies my mind with
blankness QUIERO TUS OJOS & your laughing & your
slavery . . . there be no drunken risk—i am an intimate
Egyptian—say good-bye to the marine

hi—just arrived—terrible trip—this
little man carrying a white mouse
stared at me the whole way—jesus he
was a handsome man—are there any good
lawyers around? will look you up shortly—
have to eat first

                              sincerely yours,
                              Froggy

85

A Punch of Pacifist

Peewee the Ear, whose mouth looks like a credit card—him
& Jake the Flesh—along with Sandy Bob from Pecos—
theyre leading the white elephant to water somewhere be-
tween wichita falls & el camino real—it's late in the day &
no word from Saigon is in yet—along comes jerry mc boing-
boing's daughter—Liza the Blimp—riding on a two dollar
bill belonging to Goose John Henry, negro medicine man
from Denver, who plays folk songs for kicks & speaks
french for a living—onward then when Brown Dan, the
creep cop—who likes to kill bullfrogs & whose boss keeps
saying "he's got a bad knee but you oughta see him run,
babe, you oughta see 'm run & chase them little chink lovers
when they come down the river"—anyway Brown Dan—
he comes snooping for the strangers with his flunky known
simply as Little Stick, who carries a burnt hat pin & two
pieces of kotex in case of emergency . . . they meet up with
the crew at a clearing resembling a fisherman's dwarf . . .
Jim Ghandi, the welder, is overlooking from his window—&
yells something like "aw reet ye sons a vermits—draw ye
now or shut ye mouths frever" just as the chick spreads her
legs into the intersection & lets loose with the bumble seed
grease, but nobody sneezes—she begins to yell about who
her father is, but this doesnt work either . . . her fat two
dollar bill falls dead from a bullet—"the flag of tex's ass is

upon ye" screams Jim Ghandi & the chick immediately takes to the hills—Peewee drops his cookies as up drives an XKE with Sandy Bob's cousin, Sandy Slim, who shows everybody his pictures of Nasser & says "hold it boys, i know all about these things—i used to work in the edsel factory" taking advantage of the confusion, Little Stick steals the white elephant . . . nobody notices—not even Brown Dan, who by this time is busy beating Jake the Flesh to death with a hacksaw—all in all, the situation in viet nam is very disturbing

who wants to be noticed anyway? only you,
who believes what suits you, could speak
so badly of thelonius baker—what'd he
ever do to you anyway besides get his
name in the papers? dont you know that
everybody wants to pick a moron for you—
dont concern yourself with all this
pettiness—it will all pass—think big—
youve seen the sign—all in all, tho,
youre a pretty good guy—stay clean—
dont waste your money on haircuts—see you
at the drugstore
                          your highness,
                          Gumbo the Hobo

Sacred Cracked Voice
& the Jingle Jangle Morning

go on—flutter ye mystic ballad—ah haunting & Tokay jit-
tery ye be like the mad pulse—the mad pulse of child—the
children of ring around the rosy & wandering poets over
India—the jugglers who call you by the wrong name & title
you wounded kitten—it is that easy for they know no fairy
tales . . . in the modal tuning—a pontiac is parked without
a leg to stand on—Plague the Kid—crusading in the blues
dimension, he—hitchhiking the pontiac—brooding over the
highway & searching for Joker—or perhaps the devil's eight
drummer "down with enthusiasm!" says Plague "it is all
temporary! away with it!" & Lord Randall playing with a
quart of beer—Fanny Blair dragging a judge—Willy Moore,
a shoemaker, who counts his thumbs with a switchblade
along with Sir James, the dunce, who wears a stovepipe
when he goes out on the town—Matty Groves, who secretly
at midnight tries to chop down the church steeple with
Edward, who cuts hedges for his wages & last but not
least—Barbara Allen—she smuggles Moroccan cinders into
Brooklyn twice a month & she wears a sheet—she takes
many penicillin shots "anything temporary can be used
for money reasons" says Plague & all these people—call them

what you will—they believe him—yesterday i talked to
Abner for forty minutes—he, Abner—cursed out East Texas,
tomatoes & tin pan alley—he didnt talk to me—he talked into
a mirror—i did not have the courage to crash or shatter
myself . . . when i left him, i met Puff—Puff had nothing
but bad words for unemployment, Wrigley's Spearmint &
Rabelais—i slapped myself in the face—he told me i was
crazy & my only regret being that i could not fart thru my
mouth—i walked away into a dimestore . . . what i speak
of is the crazy unspeakable microphone & great flower cele-
bration—it is not phony vision but rather friendly dark—
behold the dark—your strength—the darkness "the matri-
mony of self & spinal dream" says Plague the Kid & we buy
him a boxcar—Hysterical—melody in the Hysterical—as op-
posed to the music which offers every sound to make life
existable excpt that of silence . . . Houdini & the rest of
the ordinary people taking down puckered Jesus posters out
there on 61 highway—Midas putting them back up—in the
throne sinks Cleo—she sinks because she's fat . . . this land
is your land & this land is my land—sure—but the world is
run by those that never listen to music anyway—"enthu-
siasm is music which needs a flashlight to be heard" so says
Plague

    sorry to say baby but you ARE hung up
    arent you? you know like suppose everybody

DOES tell you youre like sabatchead
dajapeeled . . . you know what happened to him
after everybody read him—yeah he went
right up on the shelf . . . let me know if
you could use a horse tamer or a good
worried mind . . .

your meatman
Shorty Cookie

Flunking the Propaganda Course

strange men with belly trouble & their pin up girls: zelda
rat—crooked betty & volcano the leg—here they come—
theyre popped out & theyve been seen crying in the chapel
—their friend, who says that everybody cries alot—he's the
congressional one & carries the snapshots—his name is Ta-
panga Red—known in L.A. as Wipe 'M Out—he coughs alot
—anyway they walk in—it's very early & they ask for black
mongrels apiece—jenny says "why not roll 'm?" "theyre
cops!" says a little boy who just climbed a mountain &

who's learned how to smell in the circus—jenny retires to
the pinball machine—steam getting thicker—zelda rat asks
for second black mongrel—please make it hot—one of the
men, he dangles a watch in front of her face "it's late—zeld
babe—it's late" & zelda's face turns into a measle & she says
"i'm allergic"—a ringing sound & she say "oh look—that girl
over there is getting free balls"—trying to get jenny's atten-
tion, one of the men, he asks "anything bothering you?"
jenny replies "yes—whatever happened to Orval Faubus?"
& the man quickly drops the subject—his eye swollen he
pushes one of the hot mongrels down poor zelda's dress—
asks now does she wanna nother one—everybody breaks
into stitches excpt someone who's talking to a window &
jenny, who's busy racking up balls . . . the man who looks
like an adam's apple—i think he belongs to crooked betty—
he goes thru his stool—volcano—she wraps him in the na-
tional insider—everybody reads him—jenny tilts the machine
—the man's dead—just then, the congressional one, he pulls
out a luger he says a kraut give to him during the war which
is a goddamn lie, & begins to shoot up the barbecue beef
signs . . . the radio plays the star spangled banner—next
day, a young arsonist, with a turtle on his head & his hands
on his hips & his backbone slipping, sees me walking the
donkey on the east side—"saw you with jenny last nite—
anything happening there?" i say "oh my God, how can
you ask such a thing? dont you know there are starving
kids in china?" he say "yes, but that was last nite—today's

a new day" & i say "yeah—well that's too bad—i still aint
gonna tell you nothing about jenny" he calls me an idiot &
i say "here take my donkey if it'll make you feel any better
—i'm on my way to the movies anyway" it is five minutes
to rush hour—a strange transaction of goods takes place on
third avenue—the supermarket explodes from malnutrition
—God bless malnutrition

    i dont care what bob hope says—he
    aint going with you nowhere—also, john
    wayne mightve kicked cancer, but you
    oughta see his foot—forget about those
    hollywood people telling you what to do—
    theyre all gonna get killed by the indians—
    see you in your dreams
                    lovingly,
                    plastic man

Ape on Sunday

ZING & they throw him thru the door & he lands in a
truck—he gets out somewhere on the Mobile line & says
"the war's going fine—aint it paleface?" & immediately
makes a friend . . . "it's nice to have friends aint it shit-
brain?" this makes a stronger tie & both of 'm together—
they go beat up some male secretary who works for
a jockey . . . UNTOUCHABLE—they walk thru the
streets of France & poison the dogs & when they get back—
both receive medals for bravery "it's nice to have medals
aint it monsterass?" they cannot be separated these two
friends . . . they are invited to speak at religious & college
gatherings & finally become board members of the rootbeer
industry "it's nice to have all the rootbeer you can drink
aint it fishturd?" an ABSOLUTE bond that cannot be
broken . . . one day one of the friends discovers that he's
never been doing any of the talking . . . he inquires about
it but gets no response—he murders the other friend & some
young punk around town—he gets put in jail for 90 years
. . . everything wouldve been overlooked but John Hus-
ton—& i do mean John Huston—he made a Bible movie out
of it & changed all the names—also there was nothing in the
plot of course about the rootbeer stand—other'n that—it
was a full drag "i was expecting to see a bit of Mobile"—said
Princess "i was really expecting to see a bit of Mobile"—
Princess is an ape—she usually goes to movies on Sunday

look you asshole—tho i might be nothing but
a butter sculptor, i refuse to go on working
with the idea of your praising as my reward—
like what are your credentials anyway? excpt for
talking about all us butter sculptors, what else
do you do? do you know what it feels like to
make some butter sculpture? do you know what
it feels like to actually ooze that butter around
& create something of fantastic worth? you said
that my last year's work "The King's Odor" was
great & then you say i havent done anything as
great since—just who the hell are you talking to
anyway? you must have something to do in your
real life—i understand that you praised the piece
you saw yesterday entitled "The Monkey Taster"
about which you said meant "a nice work of butter
carved into the shape of a young man who likes
only african women" you are an idiot—it doesnt
mean that at all . . . i hereby want nothing to do
with your hangups—i really dont care what you think
of my work as i now know you dont understand it
anyway . . . i must go now—i have this new hunk of
margarine waiting in the bathtub—yes i said
MARGARINE & next week i just might decide to use
cream cheese—& i really dont care what you
think of my experimenting—you take yourself
too seriously—youre going to get an ulcer &
go into the hospital—they'll put you in a

ward where you cant have any visitors—you'll
go right off your nut—i really dont care anymore—
i am so bored with your rules & regulations
that i might not even talk to you again—just
remember tho, when you evaluate a piece of
butter, you are talking about yourself, so
you'd just better sign your name . . . see you,
if youre lucky, at mrs. keeler's cake festival

yours
Snowplow Floater

p.s. youre my friend & i'm trying to help you

                    collision
boss aint it awful the way
they make you look at things
as if you were inside of a toilet—
their toilet!
these sadistic nurses—they speak
to me as if i was a finger—
i lay in this bed unprotected &
the fellow next door—he must
be a Zulu—the doctors cant
stand him
& he gets no visitors—the
Sister says he's irreligious but
i just think he gags alot

boss three bodies got shipped out
this morning—Lady Esther said that
they went to the hunting ground—
Cronie said that they never were
worth much anyway & St. Crockasheet
said abracadabra—Lady Esther is
the cleaning lady & she was
mopping up the beds when i woke
up . . . there was some candle wax
on the window—Cronie said not
to touch it

there is a sign in the hall that reads "Quiet"—
it waits for no one—i think that is
what makes people different than
signs

i say to him "they'll get you"
& he say "no" & i say "& if they
dont get you, you'll get yourself"
& he say "you got bad manners &
i go to church & nobody's gonna
get me" & then some guys wearing
parachutes come in & give him
a wiff of mint & hand him a
peacock feather & then they slit
his throat . . . i looked out the

window & saw this car stop—it
had a bumper sticker saying
"Vote, Goat" & a man got out &
wiped his feet on a doormat—
he carried a book of Aesop's Fables
& then Lady Esther came in again
& cleaned up the mess—i turned
on the radio but all that was
happening was the news

boss aint it fierce the way that one
woman with the Persian monkey treated
the other woman with the Alley monkey?
Claudette came to see me last nite—
she doesnt own a monkey & she couldnt
get it—then at the same time, the nurse
came in & said "it's raining cats &
dogs outside—is it too much for you
to bear ha ha?" i couldve swallowed her

tonite i dance with Strawberry, the
bloody clothes wife—i say her head,
if necessary, would crack like an egg
& she damns me—if i thank her
then she calls me a whore so there's
no way out . . . my mind is with the kitchen
workers but when they catch spiders &

pull their legs off & laugh—it usually
wakes me up . . . i am sick of people
praising Einstein—bourgeois ghosts—
i am sick of heroic sorrow

as soon as i get out of here
i'm going to my blood bank
& make a withdrawal & go
to Greece—Greece is beautiful
& nobody understands you
there

the janitor with a glass eye—
he's all right—at least he
minds his own business—he
tells me that Shakespeare's relatives
killed his ancestors—& that now
his brothers wont read Shakespeare . .
he says that he used to ride to
church on a ox & when they sold
the church, he sold the ox . . .
the janitor, he's ok . . . Lady
Esther says that he aint never
gonna amount to much but i
never speak to Lady Esther &
what does she know about people
with glass eyes anyway?

my bosom feels like the
grave diggers have been at
it all nite . . . tomorrow
if i'm lucky, i'll have breakfast
in Heaven . . . some crazy fishhook dangles
thru my window—i might as well
get up & walk on my forehead—
i might as well lose all my tickets . . .
i wish there was something i
wanted as badly as this fishhook
wants to express itself

dear mister congressman:
it's about my house—some time
ago i made a deal with a syrup company
to advertise their product on the side
facing the street—it wasnt so bad at
first, but soon they put up another
ad on the other side—i didn't even
mind that, but then they plastered
these women all over the windows with
cans of syrup in their arms—in exchange
the company paid my phone & gas bill &
bought a few clothes for the tots—i told
the town council that i'd do most anything
just to let some sun in the house but they
said we couldnt offend the syrup company

because it's called Granma Washington's
Syrup & people tend to associate it with
the constitution . . . the neighbors dont help
me at all because they feel that if anything
comes off my house, it'll have to go on theirs
& none of them want their houses looking like
mine—the company offered to buy my house as a
permanent billboard sign, but God, i got my
roots here & i had to refuse at first—now they
tell me some negroes are moving in down the
block—as you can see, things dont look
too good at the moment—my eldest son is
in the army so he cant do a thing—i
would appreciate any helpful suggestion—
thank you

> yours in allegiance
> Zorba the Bomb

Cowboy Angel Blues

meanwhile back in texas—beautiful texas—Freud paces back
& forth—struggling with his boot & trying to finish his
Vermouth—"fraid you got the wrong idea Mr. Clap—if
was you, i'd give in & go chop those trees down for my
mother—after all, there's a little mother in all of us" "yes
but i mean why do you think i do it? why do you think i
intentionally set fire to my bed everytime she asks me to
cut down those trees? why?" "yes—well—Mr. Clap—per-
haps it is the womb calling—you know—perhaps when you
were a little boy, you heard a tree falling & the sound of it
went WOOOOM & now as you are older—everytime you
hear that sound—in one form or another of course—you
just want to—oh shall we say—light it up?" "yes that seems
logical—thank you very much—i feel to go chop those trees
down now" "ah but remember son—a tree falling in the
forest without any sound has nobody to hear it!" "yes—
well—i shall be there then—i shall not burn my bed any-
more" "good—let me know of your progress & if anything
drastic comes up—here—take these pills—by the way, you
should call your mother 'Stella' just to show her that you
mean business—oh & while youre at it, could you chop me
some firewood please?" "yes—all right—thank you very
much again—excuse me sir—are you having some trouble
with your boot?" "no—no—my leg's just getting a little

hairier—that's all" . . . get back to this beautiful texas &
dont swap that cow—Corpus Christi aflame—common
thieves—maggots & millionaires trading sons & dollars &
rolling back chumps—the black gypsy lady & Buddy Holly
himself into the tanks & voids held up to Scrawny Horizon
by Lee Marvin & the forty thieves BRILLIANT & Sancho
Panza Remembered like in an Arabic moonbook & Mal-
colm X Forgotten like a caught fish & wonder—ah wonder
just what—just what That means . . . Lovetown so pa-
thetic & the grown men crying—the winds are anchored
here & you do not disturb these tears nor rivers—you do not
take baths in the abandoned bathtubs but rather mix elec-
tric herbs & be watchdog to the Great White Mountain
. . . Funky Phaedra—in the center of a No Disturb sign &
Black Ace singing—she tries to outstare a bowl of money—
she—as they say—has one foot in the grave—the apprentice
clown, Tomboy, at her feet—he's known professionally as
Rabbit Rough & plays a homemade steel guitar—when
loaded, he really bites into it—Weep the Greed is watching
the happening from a caved-in mare & he lights a cigarette
with one of his stolen wanted posters . . , "love is magic"
says Phaedra—Funky Phaedra—Rabbit dont say nothing—
Weep the Greed says "go to it gal!" "love is wonderful"
says Phaedra "get 'm, stranger!" says Weep the Greed—
Phaedra takes off her stetson—five bunnies & a nickel shot
full of holes jump out "which way's laos?" says one of the
bunnies "some trick!" says Weep the Greed—"love is that

gliding feeling" "yipee! & i'll be a coonbong!" says Weep
the Greed "love is gentleness—softness—creaminess" says
Phaedra—who is now having a pillow fight—her weapon,
a mattress—she stands on a deserted marshmallow—her foe,
some Unitarian who's fallen off one a them high sierras &
lived to tell about it—he holds a fascist pint of yogurt "love
is riding a striped mare across the orgy plains on barbarian
sunday" screams Rabbit Rough, the apprentice clown—
this is the first thing he's said all day & now he hesitates—
Phaedra—meanwhile—is getting beaten in the fight—"sure
it is" says Weep the Greed "& then your mare ends up like
this one—then you put your arm in a sling—your feet in a
vault & then you get a job working for a camel—right?"
Phaedra—totally wiped out from the fight—she comes
crawling back—seizes Rabbit—pulls his shirt off—twists his
arm behind his back & throws him into the windmill—
Weep the Greed gets busted by the Padres & all the wanted
posters fly over the united states—the mare gets confiscated
& held without bail . . . Mr. Clap—meantime—makes an-
other visit to Freud "only rich people can afford you" he
says "only rich people can afford all art—isnt that the way
it is?" "isnt that the way it always has been?" says Freud
"ah yes" says Mr. Clap with a sigh—"by the way—how's
the mother?" "oh she's ok—you know her name's Art—she
makes a lot of money" "oh?" "yes—i've told her all about
you—you must come to the house some time" "yes" says
Freud with a martha raye type grin "yes—perhaps i will"

. . . Phaedra pounding her knuckles into a piece of water
—scratching her snake bites—a getaway car goes by consist-
ing of: three lying hunters off the Brazos River—two win-
dow peeking mothers each holding some decayed pictures
of lili st. cyr—a side order of bacon—some underprivileged
bonus babies shot full of dexedrine—a painter with a plate
on his face—one barbell—Dracula smoking a cigarette &
eating an angel—the ghost of cheetah, madame nhu &
bridey murphy all wrapped in toothpaste—a box of magic
wands & one innocent bystander . . . needless to say—
there is no more room in the car—Phaedra scowls & she
bellows "love is going PLUMB INSANE" & wine bottle
breaking—texas exploding & dinner by the sea—ship com-
manders with perfect features—theyre seen—theyre seen by
truckdrivers—the truckdrivers complain of hijacking & see
these ship commanders riding stallions into the howling
Gulf of Mexico & here comes Phaedra "love is going plumb
insane" . . . she is walking by Mr. Clap—who is smiling—
he wears his cap inside out—he's eating good fruit—HE'LL
be all right—Mr. Clap—he'll be all right

    dear buzz:
    i want the bibles marked up thirty percent—
    to justify the markup, i want free hairbrushes
    given away with each bible—also, the chocolate
    jesuses should not be sold in the south . . . one

more thing, concerning the end of the world
game—perhaps if you had some germ warfare for
it you could sell it for twice as much—things
kinda stormy round here—office in turmoil—
secretary wiped out recently—guess what happened
to the pictures of the pres? yeah well some
joker drew a earring on him in the original print
& somehow it slipped by the production staff—
needless to say, we couldn't get rid of any
of them around here that's for sure, so we had
to ship them all to puerto rico—thing worked
out ok tho—distributors down there said they
went like hot cakes . . . almost as fast as the
red white & blue hamburger sets—oh—i meant to
tell you, i think if you made the "i voted for
the winner" buttons triangle shaped, they might
go a little faster . . . by the way, i did tell you
to send the "i'm a beatles eater" handkerchiefs to
the dominican republic & Not to england—fraid you
made a little mistake there, buzzy boy! like i
said, office in turmoil—got a new kid but he fell
in the water cooler right away . . . he's suing us for
teeth damage—lotza problems

see you in the cafeteria
bosom buddy,
syd dangerous

Subterranean Homesick Blues
& the Blond Waltz

let me say this about Justine—sne was 5ft.2 & had Hun
garian eyes—her belief was that if she could make it witl
Bo Diddley—she could get herself straight—now Ruthy—
she was different—she always wanted to see a cock fight &
went to Mexico City when she was 17 & a runaway cast-
off—she met Zonk when she was 18—Zonk came from her
home town—at least that's what he said when he met her—
when they busted up, he said he never heard of the place
but that's beside the point—anyway these three—they make
up the Realm Crew . . . i met them exactly at their table
& they took 2 years of sanction from me but i never talk
much about it myself—Justine was always trying to prove
she existed as if she really needed proof—Ruthy—she was
always trying to prove that Bo Diddley existed & Zonk he
was trying to prove that he existed just for Ruthy but later
on said that he was just trying to prove he existed to him-
self—me? i started wondering about whether anybody ex-
isted but i never pushed it too much—especially when Zonk
was around—Zonk hated himself & when he got too high
he thought everybody was a mirror

one day i discovered that my secrets were puny—i tried to build them up but Justine said "this is the Twentieth Century baby—i mean you know—like they dont do that anymore—why dont you go walk on the street—that'll build up your secrets—it's no use to spend all these hours a day doing it in a room—youre losing living—i mean like if you wanna be some kinda charles atlas, go right ahead . . . but you better head off for muscle beach—i mean you just might as well snatch jayne mansfield—become king of your kind & start some kind of secret gymnasium" . . . after being ridiculed to such a degree—i decided to leave my secrets alone & Justine—Justine was right—my secrets got bigger—in fact they grew so big that they outweighed my body . . . i hitchhiked alot in those days & you had to be ready—you never knew what kind of people you were gonna meet on the road

i sang in a forest one day & someone said it was three o'clock—that nite when i read the newspaper, i saw that a tenement had been set aflame & that three firemen & nineteen people had lost their lives—the fire was at three o'clock too . . . that nite in a dream i was singing again—i was singing the same song in the same forest & at the same time—in the dream there was also a tenement blazing . . . there was no fog & the dream was clear—it was not worth analyzing as nothing is worth analyzing—you learn from a conglomeration of the incredible past—whatever experi-

ence gotten in any way whatsoever—controlling at once
the present tense of the problem—more or less like a roy
rogers & trigger relationship of which under present west-
ern standards is an impossibility—me singing—i moved from
the forest—frozen in a moment & picked up & moved above
land—the tenement blazing too at the same moment being
picked up & moved towards me—i, still singing & this build-
ing still burning . . . needless to say—i & the building met
& as instantly as it stopped, the motion started again—me,
singing & the building burning—there i was—in all truth—
singing in front of a raging fire—i was unable to do any-
thing about this fire—you see—not because i was lazy or
loved to watch good fires—but rather because both myself
& the fire were in the same Time all right but we were not
in the same Space—the only thing we had in common was
that we existed in the same moment . . . i could not feel
any guilt about just standing there singing for as i said i
was picked up & moved there not by my own free will but
rather by some unbelievable force—i told Justine about this
dream & she said "that's right—lot of people would feel
guilty & close their eyes to such a happening—these are
people that interrupt & interfere in other people's lives—
only God can be everywhere at the same Time & Space—
you are human—sad & silly as it might seem" . . . i got
very drunk that afternoon & a mysterious confusion entered
into my body—"when i hear of the bombings, i see red &
mad hatred" said Zonk—"when i hear of the bombings, i

see the head of a dead nun" said i—Zonk said "what?" . . .
i have never taken my singing—let alone my other habits—
very seriously—ever since then—i have just accepted it—
exactly as i would any other crime

the soldier with the long beard says go ask questions my
son but the shaggy orphan says that it's all a hype—the
bearded soldier says what's a hype? & the shaggy orphan
says what's a son? the taste of bread is common yet who
can & who cares to tell someone else what it tastes like—
it tastes like bread that's what it tastes like . . . to find out
why Bertha shouldnt push the man off the flying trapeze
you dont find out by thinking about it—you find out by
being Bertha—that's how you find out

let me say this about Justine—Ruthy & Zonk—none of them
understood each other at all—Justine—she went off to join
a rock n roll band & Ruthy—she decided to fight cocks
professionally & when last heard from, Zonk was working
in the garment district . . . they all lived happily ever after

>   where i live now, the only thing that keeps
>   the area going is tradition—as you can figure
>   out—it doesnt count very much—everything
>   around me rots . . i dont know how long it has
>   been this way, but if it keeps up, soon

i will be an old man—& i am only 15—the only
job around here is mining—but jesus, who wants
to be a miner . . . i refuse to be part of such
a shallow death—everybody talks about the middle
ages as if it was actually in the middle ages—
i'll do anything to leave here—my mind
is running down the river—i'd sell my
soul to the elephant—i'd cheat the sphinx—
i'd lie to the conqueror . . . tho you might
not take this the right way, i would even
sign a chain with the devil . . . please dont
send me anymore grandfather clocks—no more
books or care packages . . . if youre going to
send me something, send me a key—i shall
find the door to where it fits, if it takes
me the rest of my life

your friend,
Friend

Furious Simon's Nasty Humor

i had a dream
that the cook
leaned
& shook
his fist over the
balcony & said yes
to the people
yes the people
& he said this
to the people
"i want four cups of stormtrooper—
a tablespoon of catholic—five hideous paranoids—
some water buffalo—a half pound of communist—
six cups of rebel—two cute atheists—
a quart bottle of rabbi—one teaspoon of
bitter liberal—some antibirth tablets—
three fourths black nationalist—
a dab of lemon cock powder—
some mogen david capitalists & a whole lot
of fat people with extra money"
then the cook's helper
appeared
& cleared his throat & then he
said to the people yes the

III

people
"also we'd like a mocking bird
& some maids in milking—some raped
college students & a drenched hen—
two turtle gloves
& a partridge & a gin & a pear tree"
i awoke from this dream
in the state of fright—then jumped out of bed &
ran for the kitchen—crashed thru the door &
slammed on the light/fell on my
bended knees &
thanked God
that there was nothing new in
the ice box

dear Puck,
traded in my electric guitar for
one you call a gut one . . . you can play
it all by yourself—dont need a band—
eliminates all the fighting except of
course for the other gut guitar
players—am doing well—have no idea of
what's happening but all these girls
with moustaches, theyre going crazy
over me—you must try them sometime—
weather is good—threw away all my lefty
frizzell records—also got rid of my

parka—you can keep my cow as i now am
on the road to freedom
                    see yuh later aligator
                    Franky Duck

I Found the Piano Player Very Crosseyed But Extremely Solid

he came with his wrists taped & he carried his own coat
hanger—i could tell at a glance that he had no need for
Sonny Rollins but i asked him anyway "whatever happened
to gregory corso?" he just stood there—he took out a deck
of cards & he replied "wanna play some cards?" to which
i answered "no but whatever happened to jane russell?" he
flapped the cards & they went sailing all over the room "my
father taught me that" he said "it's called 52 pickup but i
call it 49 pickup cause i'm shy three cards—haw haw aint
that a scream & which one's the piano?" at this gesture, i
was relieved to see that he was human—not a saint mind
you—& he wasnt very likable—but nevertheless—he was
human—"that's my piano over there" i say "the one with

the teeth" he immediately rambled over & he stomped hard
across the floor "shhhhhh" i said "you'll wake up my No
Pets Allowed sign" he shrugged his shoulders & took out a
piece of chalk—he began to draw a picture of his kid on
my piano "hey now look—that aint what's wrong with my
piano—i mean now dont take it personally—it's got nothing
to do with you, but my piano is out of tune—now i dont
care how you go about it but fix it—fix it right" "my kid's
gonna be an astronaut" "i should hope so" says me "& by
the way—could you tell me what happened to julius
larosa?" a picture of abraham lincoln falls from the ceiling
"that guy looks like a girl—i saw him on Shindig—he's a
fag" "how wise you are" says i "hurry & fix my piano
willya—i have this geisha girl coming over at midnight &
she digs to jump on it" "my kid's gonna be an astronaut"
"c'mon—get to work—my piano—my piano—c'mon it's out
of tune" at this time, he takes out his tool & starts to tinkle
on a few high notes—"yeah it's out of tune" he says "but
it's also 5:30" "so what?" i say most melancholy "so it's
quitting time—that's so what" "quitting time?" "look buddy
i'm a union man . . ." "look yourself—you ever heard of
woody guthrie? he was a union man too & he fought to or-
ganize unions like yers & he dug people's needs & do you
know what he'd say if he knew that a union man—an honest-
to-God union man—was walking out on a poor hard traveling
cat's needs—do you know what he'd say d'yuh know what
he'd think?" "all right i'm getting sick of you sprouting out
names at me—i never hearda no boody guppie & any

way . . ." "woody guthrie not boody guppie!" "yeah well anyway i dont know what he'd say, but tomorrow—now if you want a new man tomorrow—like you can just call up & the union'll send you over one gladly—like i dont care—it's just another job to me buddy—just another job to me" "WHAT! you dont even take any pride in your work? i cant believe this! do you know what boody guppie would do to you man? i mean do you know what he'd think of you?" "i'm going home—i hate it here—it's just not my style at all & anyway i never heard of any coody puppie" "boody guppie, you miserable bosom—not coody puppie & get out of my house—get out this instant!" "my kid's gonna be an astronaut" "i dont care—you cant bribe me—i'm bigger'n that—get out—get out" . . . after he leaves i try playing my piano—no use—it sounds like a bowling alley—i change my No Pets Allowed sign to a Home Sweet Home sign & wonder why i havent any friends . . . it starts to rain— the rain sounds like a pencil sharpener—i look out the window & everybody's walking around without a hat—it is 5:31—time to celebrate someone's birthday—the piano tuner has left his coat hanger behind . . . which really brings me down

unfortunately my friend, you shall not get
the information you seek out of me—i, my
good man, am not a fink! none of my relatives

are or have been related to benedict arnold
& i myself despise john wilkes booth—i dont
smoke marijuana & my family hates italian
food—none of my friends like black & white
movies & again myself, i have never seen a
russian ballet—also, i have started an organization
to turn in all people that laugh at
newsreels—so: could you please stop those
letters to the district attorney saying that
i know who murdered my wife—my principles are
at stake here—i would NOT sacrifice them for
one moment of pleasure—i am an honest man
                              yours in growth,
                              ivan the bloodburst

The Vandals Took the Handles (An Opera)

to South Duchess County comes Them & Woolworth's
Fool & triumphant alice toklas, the National Bank in short
sleeves & the regulars—the sincereful regulars—House on its

final kick—still breeding & a cellarful of imaginary Russian peasant girls holding triangles—the triangles are real—House on Doomstown, an academy—a priest with his winnings from Reno coming in on a parachute . . . "integrate the house!" "only if you wish to live where youre not wanted" "then bomb the house!" "only if you wish to live there by yourself" "what do you suggest then?" "it's a pointless house—leave it alone—it is not happy within itself—it breeds disaster—it forces you to learn things that have nothing to do with the outside world & then it kicks you out there—the house dont need you—why should you be so low as to need it—leave—go far away from the house" "no, my friend, your way of thinking is called giving up" "do as you wish, your way is called losing—it's not even a way of thinking" the priest leaves with his eyes downward—he is examining the rocks but he's forgotten that his parachute has already been used once . . . alice toklas lays on a grassy knoll & blesses a flower "oh the enemy—beware of the enemy—the enemy is santa claus!" . . . the flower doesnt need her—the flower needs rain

we sat in a room where Harold, who called himself "Lord of dead animals," was climbing down from a ladder & he said "friend or doe? friend or doe?" he wore a black shawl & someone said that he experimented in the depth of mir- rors—Poncho was very startled & screamed "i'll give you a friend or doe, you freak!" & banged him with a judo chop

& stuck his head thru the ladder—"shouldnt done that" said
a very manly girl who came down the chimney "he's very
sullen but he's a good cat—does anybody want a piece of
bread?" Poncho said that he wanted a piece of kidney—i
said i wanted a piece of separate . . . the girl began to cry

in the photographs—you see the sand at Nice & Tangier &
all the medicine men looking elegant & then out come the
radar slaves—each one wanting to be an apostle & they
carry the electrograms—we call them Employment & each
one says things like "haul away ho" & "heave 'm johnny"
& "l dont dig harry james at all!" & Hefty Bore, a leftover
horror from the beat generation & a dubious health freak
saying to his bewildered birdgirl, WeeWee the Dyke, "oh
c'mon—it wouldnt cost you nothing to tell everybody that
i'm the hippest person you ever met—c'mon—i do lots of
things for you!" & WeeWee saying "but i never see any-
body—you never let me see anybody!" & then Olive, who
once started a streetfight over Carl Perkins' eyes & now
builds laugh machines for rich democrats—he brings in the
equipment & you get taken across a narrow bridge where
hundreds of tourists follow & sail lead weight records at
your feet & they place you in a giant bus horn & voices
yelling "i want that one—i want that one!" Madame Re-
member appears & she takes away your photographs & all
that's left in the outside world is your hand—little babies
bite it & mothers are screaming SCREAMING "yes—he

can have my vote—i'll vote for him any day" . . . now
youre a plastic vein—youve vanished inside of a perfect
message—historic phone calls come thru to your belly &
curious tabernacles move slowly thru your mind—hitch-
hiking—hitchhiking unashamed thru the goofs of your
brain—your ideals are gone & all that remains are the cutup
photographs of you standing in the supermarket—the bus
still runs but now you take cabs with the jungle boys . . .
Egotist shows you his diary & he says "I've learned to be
silent" & you say "youve learned nothing—youve just said
something"

the good folks around here, they got plenty of questions—
they beat elephants to death with candy sticks—"a white
bear is a crazy bear" say the thieves who really are not
thieves but rather plain people who dont expect their
friends to get sick so they'll need them—there is an illness
on the mountain & a polio lily grew out of a green purse
last Sunday—a dangerous nickel lays on the town square
. . . everybody watches to see who'll pick it up . . . TO
SEARCH IS TO NEGLECT & VIOLENT LUCK IS
STAMPEDE & there's a bunch of us around here but we
only pick up dollars

    here lies bob dylan
    murdered

from behind
by trembling flesh
who after being refused by Lazarus,
jumped on him
for solitude
but was amazed to discover
that he was already
a streetcar &
that was exactly the end
of bob dylan

he now lies in Mrs. Actually's
beauty parlor
God rest his soul
& his rudeness

two brothers
& a naked mama's boy
who looks like Jesus Christ
can now share the remains
of his sickness
& his phone numbers

there is no strength
to give away—
everybody now
can just have it back

here lies bob dylan
demolished by Vienna politeness—
which will now claim to have invented him
the cool people can
now write Fugues about him
& Cupid can now kick over his kerosene lamp—
boy dylan—killed by a discarded Oedipus
who turned
around
to investigate a ghost
& discovered that
the ghost too
was more than one person

South Duchess County importing pyramids & scavengers
by the truckload & Cousin Butch—he leaves now & tnen to
make three dollars a nite telling about the flying saucers
. . . a warmonger—Antonio—working day & nite in a
garage—he smuggles pad locks to the olympic swimmers &
hires out women for the baseball players—he's very quiet &
very fashion conscious—he knows his religious geography—
he's training his kid to be a gorilla & then he will rent him
out for people's closets—he says his right hand holds war
but his left hand holds a wet paranoid smile . . . the
peacemonger—Roach—when last seen—was chasing a train
—he says that his right hand hold peace but his left hand
was seen holding a doorknob & a meathook . . . South

Duchess County in bandages & little Lady Suntan trying to
analyze the Albino terrorists . . . South Duchess County—
pure as visions & uneducated—shall exist past the deadly
complements to it—past its lack of holidays & past the
possible

>you cant fool me—i'm too smart—you
>were on that subway train when that
>kid got knifed—you just sat there—you
>were on the street when that black car
>drove up & tossed some form in the
>river—you turned around & walked to a
>phone & pretended you had someone to call . . .
>you were also there when they castrated
>that poor boy in public—you cant fool me—
>youre not so tough—sure, you took a big
>stand on juvenile delinquency—you said to
>run all the hoods out of town—oh youre so
>brave—sure, you say youre patriotic—you
>say youre not scared to drop any H bomb &
>show everybody that you mean what you say
>but you dont say anything except that youre
>not scared to drop any H bombs—how can you
>say that my kids must learn from a good
>example? they can learn from a bad example
>just as well—they can learn from you as well
>as me—you cant have me under your thumb

anymore—not because i'm too squirmy, but because
your hands are made of water . . . when you wish
to talk to me, let me know ahead of time—i'll
have a bucket waiting . . . just because your wife
is pregnant, youve no license to meddle in mine
or my friends' affairs—ask your wife if she
remembers me

yours faithfully
Simon Dord

p.s. you probably remember me as

Julius the Honk

A Sheriff in the Machinery

Fringe—the boy lunatic—conceived on an Ash Wednesday
when Scrounge meets Suckup girl—now Scrounge, he's
twisted—he's completely wacked—ever since a midget
(who turned out to be a child actor smoking a cigar)
stomped on him like a balloon, Scrounge just aint never
been the same—it's been said that he paralyzed his home-

town soda jerk & if he didn't like you, he'd turn the jerk loose on you—to my knowledge, this never happened . . . Suckup girl—her nosejob keeps dripping & she has to carry a gardener along when she goes to parties—she is talking to Bishop Freeze, who asks her "whaja thinka that Monet painting? i mean i just got done spending five days reading Kierkegaard—alone in a room baby—just me & Kierkegaard —yeah—& the first thing i see when i come outa there is that painting—well! flip? lemme tell you did i flip? i mean did you dig the wisdom in that goddamn forehead? did you dig the crumbs in the chick's smile?" "yes i found it extremely . . . i found it extremely . . ." "monographic?" says Scrounge trying to help her out & put the make on her "yes & also i found it voluptuously interesting" when Bishop Freeze goes home, Suckup comes over to Scrounge & thanks him "dont mention it" says Scrounge who unbuttons his shirt & shows her his name signed on his stomach "had that done in Kadalawoppa last year—that's in Mexico you know" "oh that's donkey country—i know it very well— the beaches are extremely fantastic—i hear the fuzz are down there now tho" "yeah baby the fuzz come in about last Christmas—the scene now is in the jungle" "would you like to go for a ride on my stallion—we'll drop the gardener off" "yeah baby sure—then maybe we'll come back & shoot the bull" "all right—sounds wizzy—i got my gun & we can talk about Kadalawoppa & everything" "Kadalawoppa yeah & did you ever know Puny Jim down there?" "no but what about Lupe d'Lupe—did you know him—he's a retired coffee expert—comes from the coast?" "yes—oh my god—yes i did—i found him extremely uh . . . extremely . . ." "he's a natural baby—he's a natural—a meth-head but he's all beautiful—he's the one that showed me that the jungle was there" "yes me too—i found him extremely interesting" . . . nite falls now & Scrounge takes Suckup girl by the leg—she rearranges her mouth & they both go out the back door looking at the moon . . . Fringe is conceived

a greasy fat newspaper lays on Roger's counter—Roger, the owner of Cafe de la All Nite—a spanish all nite restuarant—is sad for the first time in 9 months—his mother has disappeared in Paris & he fears now that all those frenchmen might have their fun over what they think is her dead body . . . roger glances thru the facts of the fat greasy newspaper—a tiger stampede in hollywood—annette & frankie avalon found in pacific ocean—hands tied behind their backs—footage of bugs bunny documentary found in the lungs of tom mix, whom everybody thought was dead but showed up as a boxtop—rebels attack Walgreen's in Fantasia—dictator wires for more candy—U.S. sending in marines & arnold stang—in Phoenix, man eats his wife at 2 in the afternoon—FBI investigating/ bomb explodes in norman mailer's pantry—leaves him color blind—big shakeup in sports department—ed sullivan & Freshkid, a rel-

ative of Prince Rainier & visiting this country as a guest of
Cong Long, a grandson of Huey Long—seen escaping with
catchers' mitts—contact lenses & dope tablets—Bishop Sheen
very disturbed—when asked for opinion—just stated "i cant
believe it—i cant believe this could happen to ed—it mustve
been the company he's been keeping lately"—william buck-
shot junior writing oriental cookbook—is very upset that
he's lived after falling off diving board with no water in
the pool—walter crankcase arrested in Utah for lifting can-
dles—when questioned, he calmly explained that he needed
them to listen to some early little richard records—Doctor
Sponge, inventor of deer poison & snap crackle & pop
cereal—willing to take case for slight fee/ little girls spray
chancellor erhard with goose fat on his arrival from miami
—president lets embarrassing fart at banquet table—blames
it on the eggs—stock market takes worst dive in years—in
gary, indiana, colored man shot twenty times thru the
head—coroner says cause of death is unknown . . . no
good movies playing in town & only one job in the want
ads—NEEDED: a honest man to be rag picker for friendly
family—must be sturdy—preferably a basketball player—
must have a love for children—couch & a toilet—wages to
be discussed—phone TOongee 1965 . . . Roger puts down
his greasy paper & who should come in but Scrounge the
Suckup girl—it is early morning & they are not lovers any-
more—they are customers

9 months later, Fringe is born—he wears short pants—goes
to college—gets a job for a war magazine—he marries a nice
plump girl whose father is a natural winner/ Fringe meets
more & more people—he goes on a diet & then he dies

to my students:
i take it for granted that youve all read
& understand freud—dostoevsky—st.
michael—confucius—coco joe—einstein—
melville—porgy snaker—john zulu—kafka—
sartre—smallfry—& tolstoy—all right then—
what my work is—is merely picking up where
they left off—nothing more—there you have
it in a nutshell—now i'm giving you my
book—i expct you all to jump right in—
the exam will be in two weeks—everybody
has to bring their own eraser.
                        your professor
                        herold the professor

False Eyelash in Maria's Transmission

maria—she's mexican—but she's american as Howling Wolf
—"my worried mind, it annoys me! i cant take my rest! i'm
disgusting!" says her brother, who sneaks across the border
& gets drunk on skinny whores & Turkish gas—"maria needs
a shot" says King Villager "she needs a shot of a very bored
God"—the rest of the villagers sing a song that sounds like
"oh the days of forty-nine" in a Welsh accent & Adlai
Stevenson starting a riot on the mountaintop . . . maria
once nailed coffins for a living—"i will bust a plateglass win-
dow over Adlai Stevenson's head!" says her brother very
drunk on Turkish gas "i will prove to him that he too is a
masochist—i shall make him bend like a woman & wish he
was on a freight train to Frisco" —a marine with his finger
nibbled—Josephine—whose grandfather died at Shiloh—
stabbed maria once & hid her clothes—she was arrested on
an incest charge . . . King Villager, who is slowly dying
of cancer, polishes his noisy beard now & mutters "cops—
progress—american monuments" & "nothing matters" maria
has made love with a beggar recently—he was disguised in
flamboyant tinfoil—they made it in a saddlebag—she can
run a mile in 5 days point 9 & the traveling roadshow that
comes thru the town once a year respects her for it

maria's father lays dead on the hill—rich pimps—humanity
& civilization walk over his grave to show her that they
mean business . . . she is not going on any goodwill tours
this year—there is a false eyelash in her transmission . . .
there is not many places she can taste

this is my last letter—i've tried to
please you, but i see now that you have
too much on your mind—what you need is
someone to flatter you—i would do that, but
what would be the worth? after all, i
need nothing from you—you are so much
tied up in, though, that you have turned
into a piece of hunger—while the mystics
of the world jump in the sun, you have
turned into a lampshade—if youre going to think,
dont think about why people dont love each
other—think about why they dont love themselves—
maybe then, you will begin to love them—if
you have something to say, let me know, i'm
just around the corner, located by the flight
controls—take it easy & dont scratch too
much—watch the green peppers & i think youve
nad enough popcorn—youre turning into an addict—
as i said, there's simply nothing i can give
you excpt a simply—there is nothing i can take

from you excpt a guilty conscience—i cant give
nor take any habit . . . see you at the masquerade
ball

> tormentedly
> water boy

Al Aaraaf & the Forcing Committee

now the anarchist—we call him Moan—he takes us & Me-
dusa—she carries the wigs—Moan carries the maps—by noon,
we're in Abyss Hallway—there are shadows of jugglers on
the wall & from out of the Chelsea part of the ceiling drops
Monk—Moan's boy—Medusa going into a room with two
swords above the door—some removable mirrors inside—
Medusa disappears . . . Lacky, a strange counterpart of
the organization—he comes out of the room carrying a mir-
ror—both swords above the door fall down—one sticks into
the floor—the other slices him in half . . . Monk, typical
flunky & writer of eccentric gag lines to tell yourself if
youre ever hung up in the Andes—he leads us into a room

with Chinese sayings that all read "a penny slaved is a penny is a penny is a penny" . . . there is a gigantic looking glass & Monk immediately disintegrates . . . after lunch, you hear a punch of rocks & car accidents over a loudspeaker & Chang Chung—some transient & a professional extra sensual bum without any pride or shame & he's selling rebel war cries & "how to become a birth control pill' pamphlets— "invent me a signature" says Mom "i must go sign some papers concerning the zippers of truth" "zippers of truth!" says Chang Chung "there is no truth!" "right" says Moan "but there are zippers" "very sorry—velly solly—it is my mistake—it's just that i'm wearing huge shoes today that's all" "dont let it happen again" says Moan, staring down to his own shoes . . . down the hallway now in a wheelchair comes Photochick—she is the flower of Moan & she's eating a cowpie

Grady O'lady comes in—gives everybody the nod & wants to know where she can get a maid—"dig henry miller?" she asks kind of snaky like—"you mean that fantastically dead henry miller? the real estate agent henry miller?" "what you mean?" say Grady O'lady "henry's not a real estate agent—he's a cavedweller—he's an artist—he writes about God" "i'm thinking of another henry miller—i'm thinking of the one that wears a tulip in his crotch & writes about cecil b. de mille's girls . . . O'lady takes an orange out of her pocket "got this in the Aztec country—watch me now boys" she takes the orange & squeezes it very gently & slowly—then she rips it open madly & snarls & it oozes & dribbles down her mouth—all over her shirt—more—more— she's all covered in orange—Moan comes in with his art critic—Sean Checkshit & both of them—they start discussing a shipping deal "Junior Bork has just finished his novel on World War I—speaks very good for our side & we must remember not to use it for toilet paper" "i'm going to use it for toilet paper" says Photochick "explain yourself!" says Moan & Photochick explains that one person's truth is always someone else's lie & Moan he starts whipping her with his map & she starts crying & walks into a room with mirrors & blows up—"now back to this shipping deal" says Moan, who turns around to find Sean Checkshit on the floor with Grady O'lady & theyre both covered in orange "tell me more about this henry miller" says Sean "oo ah isnt it wonderful" says Grady O'lady

in Ponce de Leon land—the union leader—Stormy Leader— is on exhibition fighting a lady wrestler . . . out of his past appears Insanely Hoppy screaming & dancing Screaming— pouting "the world belongs to the woikas—the woikas—none of you want to be woikas—none of you—none of you could make it—none of you" "shut up!" says Moan, who comes in the room unnoticed "shut up—i've got a backache & any- way it's workers not woikas!" "the world is his—it's his that looks like a walrus & moves about like a walrus & has to sleep with a wife that feels like a walrus & he's forced to be a walrus for a buncha nagging kids & he goes to nagging walrus ball games & plays poker with a bunch of walruses & then he's driven into the earth & buried with a walrus in his mouth—i dare not say enough about him—he lives in his armpit & he hates you—he has no need for you—you clutter his life—you are lucky to be hanging around in his world— you have no choice excpt to walk naked—why be so honorable about it—why be so honorable about sleeping with pigs?" CRASH "put that boy in with proverb writers—but give him a bad review & say that he beat his wife & ate pork— say that he ate meat on Friday—say anything—just get him out of here till he's ready for training" . . . a lost pony express rider peers out from the trap door—he is carrying a picture of a long corridor & he sort of blows out his words when he talks "you are all fools! you cant add! you can count to a million but none of you—none of you—can see the sum total of the ground on which you stand on" Darling the Hypocrite immediately lights a fire to the floor & People Gringo pounds his fist on a book & says that rocking chair & watermelon are the same word only with different letters . . . St. Bread from the riot squad—entering with his chess pieces & a hilarious hard on & he laughs too

mother say go in That direction & please
do the greatest deed of all time & say i say

mother but it's already been done & she say
well what else is there for you to do & i say ·
i dont know mother, but i'm not going in That
direction—i'm going in that direction & she
say ok but where will you be & i say i dont
know mother but i'm not tom joad & she say
all right then i am not your mother

prince hamlet of his hexagram—sheik of unsanitary angels—
he rides on a bareback instrument—exact factor concerning
the reality of grandstand—Taj Mahal & Clytia's sundial miss-
ing—this exact factor missing . . . nevertheless—the bub-
bling under does not disturb him—Lilith teaches her new
husband, Bubba, how to use deodorant—also she teaches him
that "stinky doo doo" means nasty filth & both of these
teachings together add up to Bubbling Under Number
One . . . Obie Doesnt—whose eyes are waxed & that they
say lives in a world of his own—he keeps repeating "these
aint normal people are they? are they? oh my God—pass
the crackers—these arent normal people are they? hello hello
can you hear me?" "yes yes it's true—they are—they are the
normal people" says prince—who gives Obie a little tickle—
makes him laugh "but remember—it's like the boogie man
told the centaur when the centaur invaded the territory of
the Giant Mother Geese, 'you dont have to be around those
people'—by the way, i've heard you live in a world of your

own" "yes it's true" says Obie "& i also dont go to birthday parties" "very good" says the prince "keep up the good work" . . . about this bareback instrument—sometimes the prince is sure he's on it but not so sure he's riding on it—at other times, he's sure he's riding on it, but not so sure it's bareback—at odd moments, the prince is sure that he's riding on something bareback but not so sure it's an instrument . . . all his daily adventures, unsuccessful potatoes & other pirates try to pin him down to Certainality & put him in his place once & for all "care to arm wrestle?" say some— "youre a phony—youre no prince!" say the smarter ones who go into bathtubs & ask for the usual . . . the prince sees many jacks & jills come tumbling down "funny how when you look, you cant find any pieces to pick up" he says this usually once a day to his bareback instrument— who never talks back—most good souls dont

it is not that there is no Receptive for anything written or acted in the first person—it is just that there is no Second person

MAMMOTH NOAH & the orient marauders all on the morality rap & Priest of Harmony in a narrow costume—he's with the angels now & he says "all's useless—useless" & Instinct, poet of the antique zenith—putting on his hoofs & whinnying "all's not useless—all is very signifying!" & the insane pied piper stealing the Queen's Pawn & the conquer-

ing war cry "neither—neither" & jails being cremated & jails
falling & newly arrived spirits digging—digging their finger-
nails—their fingernails into each other . . . Goal—Hari
Cari & the Cruel Mother teasing at your harmless fate . . .
the sight of george raft—richard nixon—liberace—d.h. law-
rence & pablo casals—all the same person—& struggle—strug-
gle & your weapons of curls blowing & Digging—Digging
Everything

>   aretha—known in gallup as number 69—in
>   wheeling as the cat's in heat—in pittsburgh
>   as number 5—in brownsville as the left
>   road, the lonesome sound—in atlanta as
>   dont dance, listen—in bowling green as
>   oh no, no, not again—she's known as horse
>   chick up in cheyenne—in new york city she's
>   known as just plain aretha . . . i shall play
>   her as my trump card

i would like to do something worthwhile like perhaps plant
a tree on the ocean but i am just a guitar player—with no
absurd fears of her reputation, Black Gal co-exists with mel-
ody & i want to feel my evaporation like Black Gal feels her
co-existence . . . i do not want to carry a pitchfork

prince hamlet—he's somewhere on the totem pole—he hums
a little shallow tune "oh killing me by the grave"—aretha—
lady godiva of the migrants—she sings too . . . there are a
lot of historians under the totem pole—all pretending to be
making a living—there's also a lot of spies & customs agents
—the popes dont quit & the artists live in the meantime—the
meantime dies & in its place comes the sometimes—there is
never any real sometime & the customs agents & spies usu-
ally turn into star ice skaters on a winter vacation & they
brood about the meantime/ they usually dont know any-
body under the totem pole excpt their elders . . . San
Francisco freezing & New York neath spells of Poe &
famous barbarians "you can make it if you have nothing"
lips prince to a spaghetti dinner—wasting away on a slushy
rink—belonging to nobody & the lumberjacks are coming
"i'm searching—i'm searching for some kind of meaning!"
says Jug the Lady, an escaped werewolf—she wears a
chrome head piece & has been studying Yugoslavia for the
past ten months—she has a built-in jukebox on her motor-
cycle "your mind is small—it is limited—what kind of sense
must you need?" says prince "i want to be on the totem pole
too" she confides "the lumberjacks are coming" says prince
& then he takes out his shirt tail & begins to draw circles on
the air "there are magnets on this shirt tail & they all pick up
pieces of minute—now you see—i've got something to do—
why'n you go see this fellow—Moan is his name—he'll
straighten you—& if he cant—he knows someone that can"

one of Jug's friends, a drummer who doesnt drum but rather
just drops his sticks on the drums—comes out of the bushes
—rather a sadist type & whose entire wardrobe consists of a
marine's uniform & a washed out nurse's outfit—he yells "i'm
looking for a partner—gimme some secrets!" & then there's
two little boys playing & one says "if i owned the world,
each man would have a million dollars" & one says "if i
owned the world—each man would have the chance to save
the world once in his lifetime" . . . prince hamlet of his
hexagram—he pulls a train & makes love to miss Julie Ann
Johnson "i said gimme some secrets—i'm just the usual beer"
says this drummer & prince carves Memphis—London &
Viet Nam into the pole "there are only a few things that
exist: Boogie Woogie—highpowered frogs—Nashville Blues
—harmonicas walking—80 moons & sleeping midgets—there
are only three things that continue: Life—Death & the lum-
berjacks are coming"